EMBODIED IN LOVE

EMBODIED IN LOVE:

Sacramental Spirituality and Sexual Intimacy

A New Catholic Guide to Marriage

- CHARLES A. GALLAGHER
- GEORGE A. MALONEY
- MARY F. ROUSSEAU
- PAUL F. WILCZAK

Crossroad • New York

1991
The Crossroad Publishing Company
370 Lexington Avenue, New York, NY 10017

Printed in the United States of America

Library of Congress Cataloging in Publication Data

Main entry under title:

Embodied in love.

Bibliography: pp. 163–64
1. Marriage—Religious aspects—Catholic Church. 2. Spirituality. 3. Sex—Religious
aspects—Catholic Church. 4. Intimacy (Psychology) 5. Catholic Church—Doctrinal and
controversial works—Catholic authors.
I. Charles A. Gallagher
BX2250.E46   1983   261.8'358   83-10126
ISBN 0-8245-0594-8 (pbk)

CONTENTS

PREFACE

The Catholic Church has never had a clear and well-developed spirituality for married people, despite her long tradition of seeing matrimony as a sacrament and thus a way to holiness. Indeed, when we hear or see the words *spirituality, spiritual life, spiritual direction, spiritual books,* and so on, we usually think about monastic life, the life of celibates, of priests and nuns. We do have a well-developed monastic spirituality showing how celibates should live so as to become holy. Their way of life is virginal; their eating, sleeping, working and leisure are regulated by a daily schedule; they spend long periods of time in prayer and meditation. They take part in the liturgy every day, examine their consciences and confess their sins regularly, fast and do other physical penances. They seek gradually to become experts in prayer. And the various states of prayer have been developed and well described by the great mystics.

The thousands of canonized saints are proof of the success of monastic spirituality. But that mode of life is not for married people, not for the majority of the human race. People who are married, especially if they have children to care for, cannot spend long hours in daily prayer, cannot live a carefully regulated daily schedule, cannot easily attend Mass daily and do regular spiritual reading—not if they are to give the time and attention to each other, and to the unpredictable needs of their children, that family life demands. And yet we cannot deny that married life is a spiritual life—a life in the Spirit, a life of deep personal union with God, a life of holiness. And we cannot say that a married person's holiness comes about in spite of his marriage, that spouse and children and the daily activities of work and homemaking are somehow distractions from growth in union with God, obstacles to the spiritual life. We cannot say that married people become holy in spite of being married. For matrimony is a sacrament—one of our seven means of sanctifying grace, of that grace that is God's own life and that makes its recipients holy.

There is a puzzle, then, in the life of the Church. On the one hand, we have a constant tradition that salvation is for all, not just a select few. On the other hand, we have the fact that by far the greatest majority of canonized saints—of those held up as examples for the rest of us—are celibates. The number of canonized married saints is very small, even smaller if we leave out those who lived celibate marriages, and those who were married but then separated or widowed and became saints as single people. And there is not one married couple who has been canonized as a couple. We are not, of course, denying that there have been millions of married saints, of couples who have become holy precisely in and through their married lives. But these saints are not canonized, not publicly recognized and held up as examples. Moreover, the spirituality of the married way of life has not been well described and articulated. Married people and their counselors do not have a well-developed theology of marital spirituality to which they can turn. It is to the lack of a properly marital spirituality that this book is directed.

We do not, of course, offer here the well-developed guide to married holiness that the Church needs. Such a guide would be a huge work, the task of specialists in several disciplines of theology as well as psychology, law, and other social sciences. But we have offered an outline of the basic ideas. We assume that spiritual life is the life of grace, life in the Spirit, the life of charity, which is "the love of God poured forth in our hearts by the Holy Spirit." The spiritual life, then, is for all—not just for a celibate or monastic elite. We develop the teaching that matrimony is a sacrament, so that marital spirituality is a branch of sacramental theology. Married life, then, far from being a distraction to union with God, is an instrument of that union—an outward sign of inward grace, a symbolic cause and causal symbol of the love of God poured forth in our hearts by the Spirit.

We have tried, though, to confront in a very direct way the basic issue in a marital spirituality: we have asked what the counterpart for married people is to the celibate's expertise in prayer. Our answer is: expertise in sexual intimacy. For each of the seven sacraments has its own proper way of symbolizing the grace that it causes—baptism cleanses with water, the Eucharist nourishes with food and drink, marriage unites separate individuals in sexual ecstasy. Here we have sought to build on the Church's constant tradition that sexual intercourse is essential for a valid, sacramental, indissoluble marriage. Our main contribution, then, is a view of how sexual intimacy both symbolizes and causes the union with God that saves us from sin and death, that makes us holy by drawing us into the inner life of the triune God.

Our work began more than a year before the Synod of Bishops held in Rome in the fall of 1980. But the same thesis that we offer—the need for a marital spirituality based on sexual intimacy as a sacramental symbol—was also strongly expressed at the Synod by then Archbishop Joseph Bernardin, in a talk entitled "A Spirituality of Marital Intimacy." Basing his address on the theme of a series of Lenten talks given by Pope John Paul II in 1980, "the nuptial meaning of the body," Archbishop Bernardin first stated that all Catholics are called to a holiness that consists in intimacy with the three divine Persons. Moreover, everyone's holiness is in some sense sexual or nuptial because we are sexual beings—our bodies have a nuptial meaning. What is special to married holiness is genital sex—intimacy based on the kind of love that culminates in sexual intercourse. The content of a marital spirituality, then, would focus on the deepening of genital sexual intimacy. A marital spirituality would guide couples ever more deeply toward what Pope John Paul II calls "nakedness without shame" (Bernardin, pp. 286–288).

Our main thesis is the same as that of Archbishop Bernardin and the Holy Father. But we have also developed a theme that no other recent book on marital spirituality has taken up—the ecclesial dimension of the sacrament of matrimony. St. Paul speaks of marriage as a great sacrament in reference to Christ and his Church (Ephesians 5:32). Our Scripture makes many references to a marital relationship between God and creation, between the Lord and Israel, between Christ and his Church. We have, accordingly, emphasized that matrimony is not a private instrument of salvation for couples, but a dynamic, community-building force that looks to all mankind as possible members of the Church. In this ecclesial focus, we see love as the bond that unites people in the Church. But further, we look upon genital sexual intimacy as a transfiguring power that attracts people to the Church by transforming married people into credible symbols of the God who is love.

Our effort has been that of an inter-disciplinary team. We have tried not merely to juxtapose our views of marriage, which come from diverse vantage points and varied professional methodologies, but truly to integrate them. Thus we have not produced a collection of essays by separate, identifiable individual authors. We have, instead, tried through a series of meetings truly to integrate our ideas, and have written a book that is a genuine consensus, a common statement that thus carries all of our names.

The consensus was not easily won, for our viewpoints are quite diverse. Yet each one seemed essential to the construction of a marital spirituality that, while faithful to the Church's long and beautiful tradition, would be a genuine development of one of the neglected aspects of that tradition. Moreover, the team was—by deliberate choice—a mix of married people and celibates, of men and a woman. Dr. Mary F. Rousseau, Assistant Professor of Philosophy at Marquette University, assembled and guided the team. Her contribution is the metaphysics of the person and of sexual love essential to any correct understanding of sexual intimacy, as well as the experience of a married woman with young children. Father George Maloney, S.J., of Fordham University, provided the trinitarian theology necessary for any truly Catholic spirituality, seeing the spiritual life as a life of intimacy with the three divine Persons. Father Charles A. Gallagher, S.J., founder and long time director of Worldwide Marriage Encounter, has the nitty-gritty pastoral experience to keep our philosophical and theological feet on the ground. And Dr. Paul Wilczak, marital and family therapist in Kansas City, gave us crucial practical data and discoveries from psychology as well as the viewpoint of a husband and father.

We wish to thank each other, then, first and foremost, for making possible a book that is truly a communal effort. Our thanks go also to the American Catholic Philosophical Association, whose committee on research appointed us as their subcommittee on marital intimacy. We thank the National Council of Catholic Bishops, who provided the initial impetus and the funding for our research. We thank their Committee for Pastoral Research and Practices and its Executive Director, the Reverend Monsignor Richard Malone. We are grateful to Ewert and Kathryn Cousins, Karen Laub Novak, Katharine Rose Hanley, and John T. Noonan, Jr. for their help in planning the project. We are also grateful to Father Paul Conner, O.P., of St. Dominic's Priory in San Francisco, for several important references. And last—in place of honor—we thank those extraordinary ordinary people among whom we live, and move, and have our being, who show us the sacrament of matrimony *in vivo*—our spouses, Pris Wilczak and Ed Rousseau; our parents, our students and colleagues, our clients, our retreatants, our Marriage Encounter couples—who share with us the hope that through the sanctifying power of sexual intimacy, all may be one, as Jesus and his Father are one.

PROLOGUE:
Marriage as a Trinitarian Community

God has placed within us human beings that which sets us apart from all other earthly creatures. We are driven by an inner force to seek happiness, but a happiness that will last forever. What makes this such a haunting, bewitching power within us is that we know deep down that there can be no true happiness without love. Clothe us, feed us, satisfy all our sensual appetites, and we will painfully cry out for something more, something that will bring eternal meaning to our lives.

On the other hand, we learn from the first crying moment in infancy that being alone brings emptiness and gnawing meaninglessness. In our aloneness we frantically stretch out to possess the cotton-candied pleasures of this world, only to end up with a handful of emptiness.

Our natural experience of loneliness indicates a deeper truth, however: we are made for intimacy with God. That intimacy saves us from sin and death. God has created us for love, for he knows that love alone brings us purpose and identity. He who is love (1 John 4:8) wants us to enter into an ever-growing life of loving and being loved infinitely by the family of three loving Persons—Father, Son and Holy Spirit. In experiencing God's triune love for us, we are called into our true identity and a sense of our meaning in his eternal love. For the grace that is our intimacy with the three divine Persons enables us to love each other in an intimacy that heals our loneliness forever.

To understand why we are different from other animals, we need to understand God, who has created us to share in his very being, in a family of self-sacrificing, loving persons. The beginning and the end of our reality are found in the very makeup of God as a Trinity. God is not one objectivized Person existing in total, "splendid isolation." We must speak of God as a community or a family, in an eternal loving movement of self-giving Persons toward each other. God, before any movement of one divine Person toward the Other in love, could be considered as the Absolute *Void*—not emptiness, but rather the *fullness* of potential, that which has not yet been called forth into actuality by love. A movement outward toward another in love leads to personhood. It is not that emptiness becomes filled with fullness from the outside. It is rather that the spark of love generates the movement of a divine Person who cries out to beget himself in the image of a Son through the Spirit of love.

God's love relationships and, therefore, our own, since we are made "according to God's image and likeness" (Gen. 1:26), are not unilateral, but circular. There is a giving and a receiving, a going out and a waiting in expectant joy to be fulfilled by the response of the Other.

The Father's personhood is his love, a total, self-giving Gift to the empty receptacle, the Son, whose personhood is the loving acceptance of that Gift. The Son's love says "yes" in total gift of himself back to the Father. The Holy Spirit is the hidden, *kenotic* or emptying love, a third Person who receives his identity as he proceeds from Father and Son, *inspiring* love into them. The Spirit has his being as he unites the Father and the Son from an *I-Thou* into a *We,* a family of three Persons in loving unity and uniqueness of Persons.

CALLED TO INTIMACY

If God is love, he calls us to share his love by sharing intimately in the gift of each Person within the Trinity. God does not create us according to his image and likeness (Gen. 1:26) solely in order that we might become doers of good deeds. We sometimes wrongly seek our place in Christianity as people who have to *do* good things in order to obtain a heavenly crown in Heaven. We may even try to "impress" God and win his favor by our good works. This effort can often be a masked *egoism,* a source of pride that destroys our imaging of God's divine nature because it is the opposite of love. More deeply, though, our call to grow into the image and likeness of God is a call to live in ecstatic intimacy with God and others. Such intimacy requires a breaking down of our barriers, of our self-controlled limits to what we think constitutes our true personhood. Such love is frightening. We are deeply afraid to let go of our control over ourselves, over God and over our neighbor, and to move in utter vulnerability, availability and mutuality toward others and toward the three divine Persons.

WHAT IS INTIMACY?

Intimacy is complicated and paradoxical, and is easily confused with its counterfeits. This confusion is especially obvious in our own time, where the search for intimacy is the theme of many popular songs and movies. Since World War II, intimacy has been held up as an ideal of mental health and maturity by psychologists. Many philosophers, especially existentialists and phenomenologists—such as Pope John Paul II—have held that intimacy is what gives life its genuinely human character. Catholic theologians, too, especially in the field of ethics, have put a great deal of emphasis on intimacy, especially since the Second Vatican Council. But intimacy is not all that easy to live. And it is not all that easy to understand, either.

LONELINESS AND ALIENATION

Human persons are born as separate individuals, as unique selves, finite and incomplete. Each of us can say, for example, "I am human"—and that is wonderful, indeed. But each of us must also say (as we do when someone asks too much of us), "I am *only* human." And that is a limitation. Each of us, moreover, is only one individual, having only a tiny part of all the human existence that there is. I am myself, and that is a great good; but I am *only* myself. We are also limited in space, able to be in only one place at a time. That limitation can be terribly painful, as when we have one good friend dying in one hospital and another having a baby elsewhere. And we are temporal, so that we do not live our whole lives all at once, but only in a process, one moment at a time, moving from past to present to future. "If only I could be young again, and know what I know now" is a common lament. But of course we cannot do that. We feel a deep joy in watching our children grow to maturity. But the only way that we can experience that joy is to live through time, so that each new moment of joy brings us closer to the moment of our death.

All of these limitations, of time, space, individuality, and human nature, make for a profound loneliness in human life. Sometimes we feel that loneliness very acutely. Sometimes we don't even notice it. But it is always there, an unavoidable feature of our very existence. We do have some remedy for it, however: the sharing of each other's lives, of each other's very selves, of the lives and selves of people of other times and places. That remedy has been called by different names at various periods in the history of thought—friendship, community, communion, the social nature of man, intersubjectivity, interpersonal relationships. We shall call it intimacy. In associating with others, in loving them and sharing their lives, we somehow overcome our loneliness so that we are no longer just our isolated selves.

In a very mysterious way, by some process that is not a physical merging of two separate persons but a sharing of selves that leaves their individual identities intact, persons can come into communion with each other. Two can come to be one without ceasing to be two. Intimacy is a spiritual, psychological reality, a state of mutual understanding and love. Eating something is also a way of taking it into ourselves, making it one with us. But when we eat, our food loses its separate identity; it is destroyed by the process that converts it into human flesh, blood and bone. The people I take into my mind and heart, on the other hand, continue to exist, keep their full identity, separately from me. Thus knowing and loving enable us to truly possess, become united with, something other than ourselves. Love enables us to possess and enjoy the very self of another person in such a way that the two of us become one without ceasing to be our individual selves. We share each other's selves and identities; but those identities, far from being weakened or destroyed, are supported, affirmed, strengthened and enhanced.

A TRINITARIAN SPIRITUALITY

Our spiritual life is our life in the Spirit, the life of grace, which is the release of God's Holy Spirit within us. Grace is the image and likeness of God that enables us to live in loving intimacy with him. Through Jesus Christ, we live within his Body, the Church, in intimacy with other human beings, helping, by loving service that is truly creative, to bring all other creatures into the fullness destined by God for them. Love, therefore, is our fundamental option, our way to become truly human and hence to attain meaning in our lives. That meaning is our intimacy with the triune God, our sharing in God's ecstatic happiness. Thus the love that unites and deepens our human actions is the love of personal relationship that we call intimacy. We have been made by God for love. Basically the life God desires for us is the love of an interchange of personhoods. The intimacy of belonging to another or to others is the call to establish a communion of persons. Intimacy is thus at the heart of any Christian spirituality. It must be also at the heart of the spirituality of marriage.

As men and women, then, we have a radical decision to make in life, a commitment to who we are in God's primal plan. Do we really believe in love, and in being loved, or not? We can only come to belief in a God who loves us as he does if we first have some experience of loving and being loved simply for being the persons that we are. For that is how Father, Son and Spirit love each other. If we humans love each other only in terms of service—in what we need from, and give to, each other—we will have a false picture of God in our minds. We will think of him in terms of power and authority rather than personal intimacy. Salvation will be an impersonal rescue from evil rather than an intimate sharing of life. We must, then, in our love for each other, provide the experience of human intimacy that makes divine intimacy credible.

A TRUE INCARNATIONALISM

We must reject at the outset, if we are to formulate a true Catholic spirituality of marriage, any erroneous dualism from Gnosticism or Jansenism that might consider matter, and above all, sex, as evil.

God so loved this world and its materiality (Gen. 1:18) that his Son became totally enfleshed in matter. God creates men and women as whole persons who in marriage are to encounter each other and the triune family of God in their unselfish love. Husband and wife are not persons who "have" bodies. They *are* their bodies—"ensouled" bodies and "embodied" souls. Each is an individual, a total self, who seeks divine love. Human bodies, and physical actions, do not merely express love, for an expression of something is separate from what it expresses. People and their physical acts *enact* love, act it out. The primal symbol of sexual intercourse enacts the psycho-physical intimacy found between spouses as their participation in God's own activity in his self-giving, triune love. A true Christian understanding of marital intercourse will see bodily sexuality, not as an instrument of love, but as two whole persons seeking to attain union through self-sacrificing love. Thus intercourse does not merely express or symbolize love, express or symbolize intimacy with God. It *is* love. It *is* trinitarian intimacy, our intimacy with the three divine Persons.

Grace is not just the image of God in us, making us like Him, but his very presence in us, our very participation in his inner life. We don't just resemble or imitate God—we know him, and love him, know and love the three divine Persons as they know and love each other. So also, our actions—including sexual intercourse—don't just express, resemble, or symbolize our love. Our bodily actions are not *just* bodily; they incarnate our minds. Sexual intercourse *is* love—not just a symbol or expression of it. It is a physical and a psychological entrance into each other. In their ecstasy (literally "standing outside of themselves"), the two persons shatter their boundary limits on body, soul and spirit levels and "pass over" into an incarnate intimacy.

Here we see how wonderfully God has constituted our physical bodies, and sexuality, as a manner in which two persons in love communicate and actuate God's indwelling. Their loving presence to each other unites the deepest levels of uniqueness, along with the desire to share that uniqueness with each other. Their ecstasy is an experience of total oneness in body, soul, and spirit. Intercourse, as ecstasy, cries out for continued self-giving and receiving, for a mutual exchange of unique selves. Such oneness must continually grow by a stable existence, a life lived out in complete commitment to each other, loving as God loves, their individuality shared in constant fidelity.

To posit such a symbol of total self-giving with many partners, in a promiscuous manner, would be to act out a lie that seemingly bespeaks self-sacrificing love, without at the same time carrying through with a permanent commitment.

CONTEMPLATION IN MARRIAGE

When the two in marriage abide in love, they abide in God and God abides in them (1 John 4:18). Conjugal oneness calls for a mutual stretching in transcendence to go beyond the limits of their love already attained. As Christians, spouses believe, and experience in that faith, that God is the uncreated energy of love, bringing the two partners into an ever-increasing oneness in diversity. Teilhard de Chardin expresses well the fundamental uniqueness of love when he writes: "Love differentiates as it unites" (*The Phenomenon of Man,* pp. 264–67). This union should be the normal experience of married persons in love. At the same time that they "contemplate" their oneness in the uniqueness of the other, with a burning desire to live in loving service to fulfill the other in happiness, they mutually experience God as their ultimate Source of union and happiness and are moved to live in loving intimacy with him. Contemplative prayer is thus as necessary for married people as for anyone else who would live, and grow, spiritually.

Just as they know the need to be alone with each other to be restored and healed by their mutual love, so spouses know the need more and more for intimate moments alone with God in deep prayer. The community, experienced in their love of a trinitarian God—Father, Son and Holy Spirit—will become their strength as they seek prayerfully to build similar communities rooted in God's oneness in diversity. Their prayer alone with God will become progressively more and more a silent listening in loving self-surrender to God's inner direction. The moments alone with God will move them gently into the current of life's situation by the same deep faith, hope, and love, experienced in prayer as in work.

HUMAN LOVE—A TRINITY

Shared love converges into a single flame of love that moves, modeled on the Holy Trinity, toward the begetting of a third person, in harmony of affection and a community of love. An *I-Thou* always is open to form a *We*-community, just as the Father and Son bring forth the Spirit of love by their mutual self-surrender. Conjugal love, therefore, is always open to the third, another person, that "proceeds" from the mutual love of the husband and wife. God plants this drive toward the third within the hearts of the husband and wife so that they incarnate their mutual love in a new person who concretely and eternally expresses the ecstatic oneness that they have attained. But this drive outward toward a third is continued in the wish on the part of the spouses to give the oneness of their love to all other human beings they meet in life's situations. When children cannot be begotten directly in the mutual blood line of the parents as an expression of loving oneness, love builds other *We*-communities beyond the blood line, either through adopting children or through self-giving, creative work for the happiness and fulfillment of others.

Human love, when it is authentic, sincere and self-sacrificing, thus builds a trinitarian community. Men and women are called by God to complete each other. "God said, 'It is not good that the man should be alone. I will make him a helpmate' " (Gen. 2:18). Jesus has made it possible in the Christian sacrament of matrimony for two persons, a husband and a wife, to share his glorious life within the Trinity. In marriage Jesus gives his Spirit of love to the two persons. As they grow in deep self-giving to each other, they share in the very self-giving of the three Persons to each other and to the two of them as one in Christ. As Christ is continually dying and giving himself to the Church, his Bride, "in the same way, husbands must love their wives . . . and the two will become one body" (Eph. 5:28–32).

LOVE IS EMPTYING: KENOSIS

We are called, each of us through baptism, to a special kind of intimacy, our own personal incarnations into each other's worlds. For Jesus' new commandment, given at the Last Supper, was that we should love each other as he has loved us (John 13:34). We are called then, to make a *kenosis,* an emptying of self, as did our brother Jesus. We do this whenever we listen to each other in love and seek to understand. To give our undivided attention to another person is to do two things: it is to give of our very life, and it is to begin to enter that person's world. In this attentiveness we put aside our preconceptions, preferences, and preformed judgments, as Christ put aside his divinity. And we enter into the other person's world to experience that world as he or she does. To pay such attention is to follow the path of Jesus and to serve as he did to connect people more deeply with the presence of God. Attention to each other is the sacramental meaning of good communication in matrimony, a deeper coming to union with (Latin *cum*, with; *unio*, union) a spouse as symbol of God. But this incarnation reaches beyond marital and family boundaries to further complete the loving mission of Christ. The Incarnation, in which we are all called to participate with Christ by our baptism, forms a circle of intimacy that is greater than marriage, family, home. In accepting our baptismal mission, we join with the Lord, who "looking round at those who were sitting in the circle about him said, 'Here are my mother and my brothers. Whoever does the will of God is my brother, my sister, my mother' " (Mark 3:34–35).

TO LIVE FOR OTHERS

True contemplation of the Trinity can be measured only by love for others in outgoing, humble service. Marriage is thus a school where we learn that authentic holiness is living out, in each human relationship, our baptism of death to selfishness, and our rising with the Spirit of Jesus to live for others. Such sanctity unfolds in the routine of daily life situations. Marriage should then be experienced as a privilege in which two persons progressively learn to fall in love with each other and with God simultaneously. It becomes their basic experience, allowing their loving service to each other to project outward into a series of unending loving communities. This is the end of God's creative order and the fulfillment of Jesus' constant prayer to the Father: "Father, that they may be one as you and I are one . . ." (John 17:23).

The most significant and the prime model of the kind of love all Catholics are called to is the love of matrimony. Not everyone in the Church is called to this kind of personal communion, but all the other calls need the modeling, witnessing and prophesying of the sacramental relationship of men and women with one another in the Church, to help them to understand their baptismal call to belong to each other in the body of Christ. Matrimonial love most clearly approximates divine love. The sacramental love of couples in the Church most clearly reveals the family of the Trinity and the special mission we all have as sacramental expressions of the body of Christ. The love of spouses reveals to all human beings the intimacy and the ecstasy that all of us are called to experience. That ecstatic intimacy is God's gratuitous creating of us according to his image and likeness.

DEATH AND RESURRECTION

One of the greatest impediments preventing married spouses from growing in mutual love for God and for each other comes from the faulty current notions of love found in our modern society. The eroticism that most people call love is not *agape,* but a form of self-seeking. Married persons must be constantly on their guard against exploiting each other as objects or "things" to be possessed and used in a sensuous self-seeking. One can exploit the other selfishly by merely taking him or her for granted, believing that the other will always be there to satisfy one's basic needs. Marriage, as "stable monotony," opens up demands of sensitivity and fidelity never before experienced. These demands are a call and an opportunity for a death to self-centeredness. Such married Christians are confronted daily with the challenge of Christ to be baptized, not merely by water, but in the Spirit of Jesus. *Death is resurrection!*

One or both partners can lose the contemplative spirit of wonder and mystery and settle for mere orgasmic pleasures or other self-seeking ends. Thus married persons, seeking to grow in self-giving to each other, to God and to neighbor, will realize the need for prayer and the reception of the sacraments, especially Reconciliation and the Eucharist. In prayer and in the reception of Jesus in the sacraments they will develop gentleness and patience, in a state of constant alertness to serve each other. And they will find the divine help to preserve their ecstatic, self-abandoning desire for each other's well-being, for the intimacy of shared selves.

They will see the need to avoid selfish "possession" of each other and to develop trust in each other. They will give space and freedom to each other to develop life and talents according to God's gifts.

To support and promote each other's uniqueness will be considered a joy and a privilege.

A TRANSFIGURATION

Marriage is meant by God to be a microcosm of human society and the entire universe as these are destined to become one in the Body of Christ. As two spouses open themselves to God's personalized energies of love in their love, they have the strength to believe the transfiguring power of God, who wishes to accomplish the same unification in the world as a whole. Out of their daily brokenness, they experience a transformation into Christ. They move together and individually into a broken world to cooperate with Christ in the world's transformation by loving service. The transforming power of Jesus, the divine Physician, gives them hope to be able to transcend the brokenness and meaninglessness, both in their family and in the human situations surrounding them in their place in the world. Unsuspected energies are released in the discovery of God's transforming power in their sexual love. These energies pour out into the tasks of everyday living. No banal or monotonous task is too insignificant for God's presence to shine forth diaphanously. By cooperating with God's immanent, loving presence in each event of life, they become, more and more consciously, reconcilers of the world to God (2 Cor. 5:17–18). With new-found compassion and motherly caring, they seek to serve each unique person who enters into their lives. Diversity becomes transfigured, not into sheer unity, the sameness of an undifferentiated mass, but into intimacy. As human intimacy grows, it becomes the locus for divine intimacy. As two become two-in-one, through participating in the love of the Three-in-one, the many become a many-in-one, the transfigured Body of Christ, the Church, which is his bride.

THE EUCHARIST—A COMMUNITY GIFT

We experience God's trinitarian love for us individually in prayer, both when we face God alone in our hearts and when we discover him in communal prayer, especially in the Eucharist and other sacraments. In such moments of experiencing the triune family calling us gently into a oneness with the Father, Son and Spirit, we discover, always with new freshness and surprise, our own unique personhood that calls us to share the gift of ourselves with others. The incarnate Word images, especially by dying on the cross and by his resurrectional presence within us and inside the entire material world, the infinite love of the family of God—Father, Son and Holy Spirit, for us. Such a self-emptying love reaches its climax in the Eucharist. As we eat the glorified Body of Jesus Christ and drink his Blood, we touch the total Christ, God-Man, who brings us directly into the triune family. We touch the entire Trinity in receiving the Eucharist, and become inserted into their intimacy. At the same time, in the Eucharist, through the transforming power of the Holy Spirit, we know ourselves as uniquely different from the three divine Persons. In our unique *personhood* discovered in the triune love of Father, Son and Spirit, we become empowered to return the gift of ourselves back to God.

We find, through the fervent reception of the triune God in the Eucharist, the power to go from the banquet table outward into our daily living to extend the family of God into other loving communities. To the degree that we have knowingly received the divine power of the Trinity in the Eucharist, to that degree we experience the power that drives us outward toward other communities to be the Eucharist, bread broken, by giving ourselves to all whom we meet. We do not merely do what Jesus did in His self-giving, encountered in the Eucharist. We now have Jesus and the Father abiding within us by their Spirit of love. This Spirit empowers us to do that which would be impossible for us to accomplish alone.

St. Paul saw immediately the application of the Eucharist-community to marriage: "Husbands should love their wives just as Christ loved the Church and sacrificed himself for her to make her holy" (Eph. 5:15). The principal fruit of the Eucharist, "the communion in the Holy Spirit," is an intimate union of all men and women in the Mystical Body of Christ. This body is the central scope of the Eucharist, the union of all faithful through the mutual union of each individual with the Holy Trinity. The Eucharist creates the unity of all who participate in the same Bread of life. How much more, then, should married persons, husbands and wives, be able to extend the Eucharist into their conjugal love and relationships with their children, other relatives and friends! By their experience of the triune family of God living within them, they gain the power to "bear with one another charitably, in complete selflessness, gentleness and patience. Do all you can to preserve the unity of the Spirit by the peace that binds you together" (Eph. 4:2).

BUILDING THE BODY OF CHRIST

Love begets love. Such love of God, poured into the hearts of husband and wife, pours into their children and friends. The spouses begin to experience Church now as their own creative, loving actions to bring the Body of Christ into greater resurrectional glory and fullness. The spouses in their social relationships see the same unity-in-diversity that they experience in their conjugal oneness. Thus they strive to cooperate with the Spirit of Jesus to build his Body. They live in the power of the triune community experienced within them and within their family, that enables them to build a similar *I-Thou* in a *We* community in all social relationships. No longer is God to be found by escaping from worldly involvements; by "inscaping" into the very heart of matter spouses become, with the God of the universe, cocreators of new life in the world. They enflesh, for an unbelieving world, the truth that "God is Love, and he who lives in love, lives in God, and God in him" (1 John 4:16).

CHAPTER I

SEXUAL INTIMACY, THE KEY

it's not two ones are two
but two are halves of one

e e cummings

The key to marital holiness is intimacy of a special kind—
that achieved, and enacted in, sexual intercourse. We mean, of course,
something more than what lawyers refer to when they ask a witness,
"To your knowledge, were the defendants ever intimate?" In legal
language, intimacy is sexual intercourse in a purely mechanical sense—
without any reference to love or personal concern. But we are using
the term in the sense in which recent psychiatrists use it—those of
the school of Eric Berne, or of the psychologist Erik Erikson. We
are referring not just to a psychological closeness, to two people's
sharing of a private little world where they exchange secrets and
stroke each other, but to the honest and open, game-free, nondefen-
sive sharing of each other's psychological selves. That kind of intimacy is established only by altruistic love, by a mutual concern for,
and enjoyment of, each one's true personal goodness. It doesn't just
happen during sexual intercourse, but is the more or less constant
state in which sacramental spouses live.

Such intimacy presupposes that a person has a self to share—a
well-developed and mature identity, sincere convictions, strong and
clearly identified emotions. It presupposes that a person is secure in

21

his identity, and that he trusts that his intimate friend does indeed care for and enjoy his identity. Such a trusting exchange of selves in altruistic love constitutes intimacy; the medium of exchange may or may not be sexual intercourse. If intercourse is the medium of exchange, the intimacy is that proper to the sacrament of matrimony.

Pope John Paul II's phrase "the nuptial meaning of the body" captures what we mean here. Each human body—that is, each person's very self, matter animated by spirit—has a nuptial meaning. Our sexuality—whether we are male or female—is not an incidental characteristic, like the color of our eyes or our height. These can be overlooked when we think about the holiness that is the purpose of our lives. But our sexuality marks every cell of our bodies, as well as our feelings, minds, and wills. Men and women have nervous systems that are slightly different in their structure. Thus our ways of perceiving reality—of seeing, hearing, touching—are somewhat different. Our ways of believing, hoping, and loving are also somewhat different. Our ways of coming to intimacy are thus different— our intimacy with each other and our intimacy with God.

We do not wish to overemphasize these differences and imply that men and women belong to two different species. If we were that different, there could be no communication, and thus no intimacy, between us at all. The differences between the sexes are not like differences between a bird and a fish, or even between two different breeds of dogs. Sexual differences among humans are differences within the same species so that men and women are related to each other; the sexes are complementary, not just different, but related. Human nature is not complete in a single person but needs to be completed, complemented, by some sort of union with a person of the opposite sex.

And yet human nature is in a way whole in each person, and basically the same in each person. Each person, whether man or woman, has everything it takes to belong to the human species instead of any other, especially the capacity for intimacy with God in and through intimacy with other human beings. No being of any other species has those qualities. They are specifically, distinctively, human. No fish or bird, mammal or reptile, can even conceive of intimacy, let alone achieve it. But human beings of both sexes can. Human nature is basically the same in men and women. Both have equal dignity, equal rights, equal responsibilities. Neither is more or less human than the other.

But the differences are there, and they are important. They are not, of course, the stereotypes predominant in our culture—that women are intuitive, emotional, weak and passive, while men are rational, tough and invulnerable, natural leaders. People of both sexes, because they are people and not some other kind of animal, are capable of intimacy, and so both are capable of developing the traits that intimacy requires. Thus both men and women need to be intuitive and rational: both must have deep and strong but well-controlled emotions, including sexual feelings; both must be strong and courageous, able to take initiative, ready to follow someone else's lead when that is the way to intimacy. But there are distinctively masculine and feminine ways of developing, and exercising, these traits. There is something about men—all men—which women do not share. And there is something about women—all women—that men do not share. And these natural sexual differences are not trivial. They affect our humanity at its core, our distinctively masculine and feminine ways of coming to intimacy, and to intimacy with Intimacy.

The nuptial meaning of the body, then, refers to these innate sexual differences that make us incomplete in our very selves until we come into intimacy with people of the opposite sex. To be a human being is to be naturally made to find happiness and fulfillment, completeness as a person, in some sort of nuptial intimacy, to achieve the nuptial meaning that is born into our bodies. Thus all of us, celibate or married, are called—by our creation in the image of God—to enjoy intimacy with our sexual complements. The nuptial meaning that lies in the make-up of the human body, of human persons, means that every encounter, every relationship, is to be in some sense marital—not genital, of course, but an instance of intimacy involving the complementarity of the sexes. Human bodies, human persons, human relationships are all nuptial—called *nuptial* because there is something about all kinds of intimacy that is clearest in the relationship of husband and wife, clearer than in any other relationship. That something is not, obviously, genital, expressed through sexual intercourse. But it is the core of every truly human contact. Whatever it is, the special character of nuptial intimacy is meant to be present in all human relationships—those between parent and child, student and teacher, friend and friend, priest and penitent, pastor and congregation.

What is this something, this special characteristic that is more clearly and dramatically evident in marital intimacy, but is also the main feature of every other human encounter that measures up to what a human encounter ought to be? It can only be the complementarity achieved in the ecstatic abandonment of one's own person to the person of another. That self-abandon is what spouses experience in a highly dramatic moment at orgasm. And that self-abandon is what must be present, less dramatically, perhaps, but just as really, in every human contact. To the extent that we fail, in our dealings with any person, to cherish and be aware of that person's uniqueness, to be devoted to that person's needs to the point of generous self-sacrifice, to enjoy our communion with that person, to put our feelings as well as our free wills into that devotion and enjoyment, we fail to really love that person as Jesus loves us. But when we do love someone as Jesus did, we share the New Covenant with that person. For the New Covenant is a nuptial covenant based on the new commandment that Jesus gave to us at the Last Supper—to love each other as he has loved us. When we fail in loving anyone, even a stranger, we fail to live out the nuptial meanings of our bodies, to be fully the man or woman that we are born to be. We miss out on the intimacy of intimates with Intimacy that is our holiness and salvation. We violate the sacrament that is the Church. We leave our own incompleteness incomplete, our emptiness unfulfilled.

The vocations of marriage and celibacy in the Church are thus basically the same—to achieve nuptial intimacy with every person we meet, allowing our sexually differentiated selves to complement each other in passionate, ecstatic love. Spouses enact that love in all the details of their daily life together, culminating in sexual intercourse. But all of us act out the same kind of passionate, self-abandoning love when we do what is appropriate in contacts with other people—making honest business transactions, cooking for a sick neighbor, voting for the nuclear arms freeze.

Matrimony, though, is a sacrament, meant to be a highly visible and credible manifestation, and cause, of the intimacy of intimates with Intimacy that is the Church. Celibacy and consecrated virginity are not sacraments; neither are the relationships of married people to those who are not their spouses. But all of these other meetings between persons within the fundamental sacrament of the Church, the celibate, virginal ways of life and the encounters of married people with friends, relatives, and so on, are meant to be marked by the same basically nuptial intimacy that is so dramatically clear in marital intimacy. We are all, always, to love each other with passionate self-abandon.

Marriage sets the norm for all of Catholic spiritual life. Thus the challenge to celibates and virgins, the challenge to all of us in our nonspousal dealings with children and friends, is great indeed. But our opportunity is also unspeakably great. In all of our human encounters, we are to be credible symbols of the Trinity. And we become those symbols by being each other's intimates, by living a passionate, self-abandoning concern for each other in every moment of meeting. We Christians are to be remarkable, noticeable, credible, for the way we love each other, and our love for each other is our intimacy with God. In our intimacy we build the Church—we, ourselves, are the Church, and we attract the unchurched by making such intimacy credible to those who do not yet share it.

The nuptial meaning of the human body, and thus the potential intimacy of every meeting between human persons, is profound indeed. The great mystics have always known this fact. They experience something in the higher states of prayer, a passionate, ecstatic intimacy with God that is of a special delight and intensity. All of them, in trying to describe that intimacy, fall back on the language of marital love, of sexual intimacy. They are right to do so, and their language is not just a figure of speech. The love that Mother Theresa feels for the people she cares for, the exultation she experiences in prayer, are not just metaphorically but really sexual, really nuptial, even though genital sex is not her way of enacting her love.

And in our Scripture, both Old Testament and New, the relationship between God and men—between the Lord and Israel, between Christ and his Church—is most often presented in nuptial language, as the relationship of bridegroom to bride. The Scripture uses other images, to be sure—God is our shepherd, our king, our healer. But the nuptial imagery is not on a par with the rest. It is the primary imagery, and it is not purely figurative. Our intimacy with God is truly nuptial, and is achieved only in our truly nuptial intimacy with each other. Celibates must make nuptial intimacy credible without the drama of sexual intercourse. But celibate love must be just as ecstatic, just as passionate, just as nuptial, as marital love. For we are nuptial beings in our very make-up.

Throughout the history of the Church, the spiritual life has been a life of intimate personal closeness to God. The term *spiritual* reflects this idea: it is not opposed to *material*, in such a way that our spiritual life is one of withdrawal from the world, detachment from our own bodies, and rejection of pleasure and other physical delights. Our *spiritual* life is our life in the *Spirit*, our life of friendship with the Spirit of Jesus, with Jesus Himself, and with the Father. It is our life of intimacy with the Trinity. That life has always been deeply incarnational, not a life of flight from the world or from our own bodies. Our spiritual life is everything we do with a loving intention, including obviously material actions like eating and touching. We can see this incarnational aspect of Christian spirituality in the Ascension: Jesus did not see his body as a used-up, worthless tool to be discarded once he had finished his job on earth. It was a cherished part of his very self, taken up to Heaven for all of eternity.

Thus all Catholics have basically the same goal or purpose in life: married, celibate, consecrated, or ordained, we are all called to holiness, to become saints, to fulfill the will of God, to attain Christian perfection. All of these phrases speak of the same reality, our intimacy with God. And that intimacy, according to the basic theme of our Scripture, is a nuptial one. It is the life of charity. But we who live that life are human beings, not disembodied spirits. Hence our holiness, whether we are married or celibate, is by way of a love that is humanly whole—a love that involves our bodies, our physical activities such as work, our emotions, and our sexuality.

It is a mistake—and a common one—to say that the difference between marital and celibate spirituality is that the former is sexual while the latter is sexless, for both must be humanly whole. Celibates do not enact their sexual passion in sexual intercourse. But intercourse is only one way of acting out human sexuality. Celibates have other ways to love, ways that are as passionate as genital sex, as ecstatically self-transcending.

It is also a mistake, and a common one, to say that celibate spirituality is a superior spirituality to that of married life, precisely because it is sexless, and that married people can find only a deficient intimacy with God because they are distracted from contemplative prayer by sexual desire, sexual pleasure, and the practical concerns of family life.

For sexuality is more than a natural part of our very selves. For Catholics, genital sex is a sacrament, an instrument of grace, not an obstacle to it. What, though, is the special character of the kind of intimacy found only in marriage? In order to see this special character, we need to look more carefully at human love, and then at sexual intercourse as a special way of acting out love. *Love* is a much abused word, one with many confusing meanings and connotations. We love almost anything—from pizza to music or money—as well as people. Our "love" of people sometimes means enjoying them, sometimes using them—as when teenagers lure each other into intercourse in order to reassure themselves of their own self-worth. Sometimes "love" is dispassionate service, sometimes dreamy romance. This last meaning is the usual one in our culture, the theme of many movies and TV programs and popular songs.

We are defining love very precisely as the willing of someone else's personal goodness for his or her own sake, rather than for any use or pleasure for ourselves. We are not referring primarily to a feeling, but to willing—a decision or choice. Love is thus under our control—something we choose or decide to do. Such love can be dispassionate—as when we send our annual check for taxes, without any feeling for those who will be helped by various government programs. Such love can also be quite passionate, as the love-making of a couple who are very aroused sexually. Such love may even be against our feelings, as when we decide to do something that is painful but good for a person, such as consenting to a painful operation for a crippled child. But essentially love is a choice—it doesn't have to feel good in order to be love; if it does feel good, that is a bonus.

The kind of love that establishes intimacy is altruistic or benevolent, the willing of personal goodness to someone other than ourselves, for that other person's sake. This kind of love requires the psychological act of identification, an act by which we use our imagination to see the person we love as our other self. We put ourselves into his shoes, try to see the world from his point of view, and then wish for him what we would wish for ourselves. The result is that we identify that person's happiness as our own, enjoying as our own fulfillment what is in fact good for the one we love. One who loves this way does not love *as if* the other were himself. He loves his beloved *as* his other self.

This kind of love—and no other—leads to intimacy. It brings two people into oneness, into communion. The tie that binds them is their joint possession of a common good—whatever good the lover wishes for the beloved. That good is obviously the beloved's good, something that adds to his welfare or happiness. But the lover has also made that good his good, too, by his choice to identify with the beloved, by seeking the loved one's good as his own.

Such communion, which we are calling *intimacy,* is weakened and destroyed by selfishness. Let us look for a moment at the paradoxical nature of these two attitudes that we humans can take toward each other. We begin our lives without being able to differentiate ourselves from what we cling to, our mothers. As we live and act, we develop a sense of ourselves as separate and seek to heal our solitude by forming links, or bonds, with the people and things around us. But there is a paradoxical fact about these links: we can really possess, or be linked to, things and people only if we respect their own integrity. This holds even for material possessions. For example, if I am to own a car in some way that will benefit me, I have to care for it. It has a certain integrity, a structure of its own, which I must respect. If I don't, if I treat the car wholly according to my whims and neglect its maintenance, I soon find that I have no car at all, or at least none that can serve my needs. But if I take the time and energy to comprehend and maintain what it needs, I am rewarded with a fulfillment of my needs—an efficient and comfortable mode of transportation.

We can draw a parallel with people. If I am to attain communion with other persons, I must respect their integrity, the fact *that they are persons* in their own right, with uniquely individual dignity, destiny, freedom, and needs, just as I am. They are not objects to be used for my own benefit. Such respect for the dignity and integrity of others is necessary for love. For I must love other persons as myself. If I don't, if I selfishly use people wholly in accord with my convenience, if I neglect, damage, or even destroy their personal good, I soon find that I have no other person at all, or at least none that can be my friend. In order to enjoy the happiness of others, to be in communion with them, I must let their happiness exist. I must protect it, work for it, put myself at its service. There is a double paradox here: love of others is fulfilling to the one who does it, because it brings those beloved others into communion or intimacy with him. But selfishness is defeating to the one who does it because he cares for, and thus possesses, no one's goodness but his own. And anyone who loves his neighbor enjoys intimacy not only with that neighbor, but with the three Persons who come and take up their abode in him. But one who chooses not to love comes into communion with no one but himself. He is confined to his own isolation.

The nature of love, then, decides the quality of intimacy. The reason why I as a lover find fulfillment is that in the mysterious realm of human spirit, I need not lose anything of my own when I step out of myself in altruistic love to care about the good of another. I remain myself; I keep that special set of thoughts and feelings which constitute my identity as a person. And yet, I come into communion with the unique personhood of the one I love. As he or she comes to dwell in my mind and heart, something increases the personality that is already there. The welfare and happiness of the beloved become mine by my simple decision to make them so, to care for them.

Thus am I truly fulfilled, filled full, by extending my own identity into that of the person I love. And there is a parallel reason why the selfish person remains lonely, empty, not filled full, unfulfilled. When I am selfish, I have no care for the welfare and happiness of another; I seek only my own. Since that is all I seek, that is all I have; I am never satisfied. No one comes to dwell in my mind and heart, for these are closed inward on themselves. I admit no one to dwell in my mind, for it is full of me; I allow no one else's good to become mine, for I do not make the decision by which it does so become, the decision to care for the other. I have no friend, then, to be my other self. I am deeply empty and alone.

The difference between these two attitudes was made dramatically clear in the recent Academy Award movie, *Ordinary People*. The father, Calvin Jarrett, truly loved his son—cared for him with a generous, altruistic, desire for his welfare. He identified with his son, trying to see the world from Conrad's point of view, and then wished for Conrad what he would wish for himself if he were

Conrad—mental health, as that could be brought about by psychiatric treatment. Furthermore, Calvin then took Conrad's new mental health as a good of his own—Conrad's happiness was *his* happiness, simply because he chose to make it that, to care about it and enjoy it when it came about. He was happy because Conrad was better.

Conrad and Calvin, as a result of Calvin's love, thus shared a common good. The boy's new mental health was certainly his—it was in him, as his health. But it was also his father's, because the father had chosen to make it his own good and fulfillment. By jointly possessing a common good—Conrad's health—the two persons, father and son, came to be one with each other. And yet they remained two, each keeping his full separate identity. Calvin gained something—his son's happiness— without losing anything of his own identity and well-being. That is what fulfillment is, the filling full of an emptiness, the increase of one person's existence by the possession in love of some other person's existence.

Paradoxically, though, such fulfillment can only come about through genuine love—the benevolence, altruism and generosity by which we wish to another, for that other's sake, what is good for him or her. Conrad's mother, Beth Jarrett, is a clear example of the selfish, possessive, utilitarian attitude toward people that not only damages or destroys them but also defeats the fulfillment of the person who takes that attitude. Basically, the difference between father and mother in *Ordinary People* is that Beth Jarrett was not interested in her son for his sake, but for hers. She did not identify with him, trying to see the world from his point of view and then wishing to him what was good for him, for his sake. Nor did she choose to locate her own happiness outside herself, in her son's well-being. She failed, in other words, to decenter her concern, to focus it away from herself. She remained self-centered, her attention and energies on herself, looking to other people only to the extent that they promoted what was good for her.

Her selfishness is evident in her wish for Conrad to do well on the swimming team. She did not want his success for his sake, as something good for him, but for her own, for the prestige that it gave her among her friends. She never even considered whether swimming was good for Conrad, nor whether anything else was, either—including meaningful conversation with him about his problems. She wished, in fact, to send him away to boarding school rather than undertake the hard task of identifying with him so as to meet his needs and locate her own happiness in his. The result was a terrible loneliness—for her, not just for her son. Beth and Conrad never came into any kind of communion or intimacy. She was left alone in the solitude that we are all born into. She defeated her own fulfillment and happiness by her failure to love, by not making the choice she could have made to identify someone else's good as her own.

The intimacy between people that results from unselfish love is also the intimacy with Father, Son and Spirit that is the life of grace. But when spouses enjoy such intimacy, enacted in genital sex, their love is a sacrament. Let us look, then, at the special sacramental character of marital intimacy.

Basically, any sacrament is an outward sign of inward grace, a physical carrier of a psychological reality. Sacraments are symbols. But they are not *just* symbols, not mere symbols. They are causal symbols, or symbolic causes. They effectively produce what they symbolize—grace, the divine life of trinitarian intimacy, in us. But they cause grace precisely by symbolizing it. Thus the accuracy of the symbol is all-important in any sacrament. In baptism, for example, the symbol is one of washing, cleansing, dissolving and removing sin and its effects. Thus we do not baptize with materials that signify something else—soup, for example, or dust, or oil. We baptize with something that cleanses, water. But the cleansing action of the water is not *just* a symbol—it is a real, effective cleansing. The action really does what it says it is doing. Our sinfulness is not just covered up, or overlooked by God in some pretense that it isn't really there, or doesn't really matter. No, our sinfulness is really cleansed, dissolved, washed away. This symbolic causality, or causal symbolism, is the core reality of any sacrament.

All of our seven sacraments, then, somehow symbolize, and in so doing bring about, grace—our intimacy with the trinitarian intimacy, in and through our intimacy with each other. All of our sacraments are ecclesial—they either begin or strengthen or restore our membership in the Church, the intimacy with each other that is also our intimacy with the three Persons. But we have seven sacraments, not just one. To understand them all, we must understand what is the special, distinctive way in which each signifies and causes the intimacy of an intimacy (the Church) with Intimacy (the Trinity). Our next question, then, is: what is specific to matrimony? How, exactly, does matrimony signify the divine life in a way in which none of the other six sacraments can do?

The answer is in the special character of orgasm, of sexual ecstasy. For sexual intercourse is the heart of the symbolism of the sacrament of matrimony. While theologians over the centuries have had long, involved disputes over what constitutes a valid, licit and sacramental marriage, there are some constants in the Church's tradition. And sexual intercourse has always been considered essential to the sacrament of matrimony.

A formal ceremony of vows was not always required; a sort of common law marriage was also practiced, for many centuries. Couples simply took up a common life which, once consummated in sexual intercourse, was considered a valid sacrament which bound them exclusively to each other for life. The vows that are required now merely ritualize a reality that is more basic, namely, the fact that a sexual union is a special kind of intimacy symbolized, and achieved, in sexual intercourse. In fact, vows alone are not enough. Though a couple is legally married as soon as the vows are said, until their marriage is consummated in sexual intercourse, it can be dissolved.

Furthermore, involuntary sterility has not been considered an impediment to a valid marriage, but impotence has. When sterile Catholics marry, their sexual union constitutes a permanent and exclusive sacramental bond. Others may marry, enjoy a normal fertility, and later become sterile; when they do, they don't cease to be married. But it is otherwise with impotence. Primary impotence, a permanent inability to have intercourse, is an impediment to the sacrament of matrimony. There is something about sexual intercourse, even when it is not reproductive, that is so central to the sacramental symbol that where that something is present, matrimony can be recognized, and where it is not, there simply is no marital bond. What is there about sexual intercourse that makes it an epitome of marital intimacy?

When intercourse is an enactment of the kind of love that produces intimacy, orgasm is a moment of supreme generosity, of a psychologically unique altruism, of an intimacy that is as complete as any can be. Any loving action requires some degree of self-forgetfulness, of self-abandonment, of putting ourselves into the background in order to focus our attention on the person we love. We must pay attention to him or her in order to make our actions suitable to that person's needs. By way of contrast, consider children. In the selfishness that is natural to immature humans, when they select a gift for a friend, they choose what they themselves like, whether the gift is suitable to the friend or not. But in order to really love, we must turn our minds toward our beloved. If fact, when we notice our children selecting gifts according to their recipients' tastes, we realize that they are growing up, beginning to love in a somewhat unselfish, adult way.

In spite of knowing that we must center our attention on the one we love, instead of on ourselves, however, we usually do keep some degree of self-awareness. Even in the ecstasy of first romance, when we become so absorbed in our beloved that we don't notice the passage of time, or the lighting of a second cigarette before the first one is finished, we do usually know in some fringe of our minds who and where we are and what we are doing. But in the moment of orgasm, the last shred of self-consciousness is gone; we *do* forget who and where we are and what we're doing—at least for one ecstatic moment.

The same is true of self-control. When we love someone, we must in some degree give that up, give our freedom over to that other person; we must not let our words and actions be random, or focused on our own desires to speak and act. We must direct them to the needs of the one we love. We must, in other words, pay attention to what we say and do, control our words and actions, making them what we deliberately, freely, and lovingly, choose them to be.

But in the moment of orgasm, the last shred of self-control is gone; our freedom is so completely abandoned to the person we love that we find ourselves speaking and acting in ways that we cannot, and do not wish to, control. We babble and scream, lovingly abandon our whole self, body, mind and heart, into the hands of the one we love, as completely as we can. Sexual intercourse, then, is the body language *par excellence* of generous, altruistic love and of the intimacy, the passionate, ecstatic, altruistic communion that such love produces.

Thus there is a good reason why the Church makes sexual intercourse central to the sacramental symbol of matrimony. In no other human action do persons so dramatically give themselves to each other, and thereby become totally themselves. Such ecstatic love resembles the inner life of God, in which three Persons give themselves over to each other in an intimacy that is infinitely perfect. And the symbol is not *just* a symbol; it is an effective cause, so that intercourse, when it is an enactment of charity, of a loving way of life, not only resembles the divine intimacy, but effectively causes us to be drawn into it. We become God's intimates, too, by the sacramental power of our own intimacy. The power of the experience of falling in love as a stimulus to enthusiastic generosity and self-sacrifice is as nothing in comparison to the power of regular and satisfying love-making over the years of a marriage. In this way of life we gradually learn to love altruistically. We find, at last, that it is easy, not difficult, to love, with a tender concern, the person with whom we share sexual ecstasy.

If a symbol is to be an effective cause of what it symbolizes, and thus if intercourse is to be an instrument of divine grace, the symbol must be accurate. It must really say what it purports to say. Otherwise we have a countersign, a blasphemy instead of a sacrament, a barrier to rather than an instrument of the grace which saves us from sin and death. And herein lies the key to marital intimacy, and thus the key to a marital spirituality that would be properly sacramental. Marital spirituality needs to be correctly rooted in sacramental theology, which makes the life of Catholic spouses a special realization of the eucharistic community in which Christ the Bridegroom truly becomes one flesh with his cherished Bride, the Church.

The first requirement for an accurate marital symbol—for intercourse that really is an enactment of the generous love that it purports to be—is one that every married couple soon learns: that the act of making love, if it is to be successful (regularly and mutually satisfying) cannot be done in isolation from the enactment of altruistic love in the rest of their life. In fact, love-making is not even the usual way, let alone the only way, in which couples express their love for each other. When it does come to be so, when it is not the enactment of a more comprehensive sexual tenderness, it can become frustrating, irritating, even repulsive.

Masters and Johnson have confirmed this fact in their research. We can criticize their methods if we wish, but they have some very helpful knowledge of the physiology and biochemistry of sexual intercourse. And their research has convinced them that sex works best and is most satisfying, when it is exercised in the context of a loving way of life. In Virginia Johnson's wonderful phrase, the key to biologically successful love-making, to orgasmic sexual activity, is the "exchange of vulnerabilities"—the daily exercise of the mutual trust that enables couples to gradually reveal their deepest, most important psychological selves to each other. Such trust makes for a constant high level of sexual desire, and for the relaxed love-making that allows ecstasy to take us by surprise.

On the other hand, when desire is suppressed instead of fostered; where there is no trust, but only suspicion; where partners exploit each other through reactive power plays rather than living out a tender mutual responsiveness; where each is anxiously seeking to get pleasure rather than to give it—the love-making fails, even in purely biological terms. One spouse (or both) will not become aroused, or will become aroused but not reach a climax, will not experience the self-abandon of orgasm. Such unloving attitudes make for tension and self-consciousness, for women who strain for control and men who strain to resist it. And this competition leads to the problems that often require sex therapy: impotence, premature and/or retarded ejaculation, inhibited sexual desire, orgasmic dysfunction, and vaginismus. Sacramental sexuality, then, must be an enactment of mutual generous, tender, self-sacrificing concern. Only then can it be an accurate symbol that can be an effective cause of grace. And that tender concern and self-abandonment must be the mark of daily life, of all those husband and wife encounters, trivial and profound, in which they gradually weave the web of their intimacy.

As a matter of fact, those of us who have been in love, or have seen people who are in love, have experienced this genital sexual intimacy in a very direct and powerful way. Lovers feel an utter fascination with every detail of a person other than themselves. They "quarrel" over where to go and what to do on a date, which records to listen to, what kind of food to order—not because they cling to their own preferences, but because each truly prefers the desires of the other. They become so absorbed in each other that they don't notice the passage of time, seldom feel tired, miss favorite TV programs, sometimes forget to eat. What they feel is the beginning of sacramental sexuality, of self-forgetfulness and self-abandon, energized by sexual feelings, that symbolize, and draws them into, the perfect self-abandon of the three divine Persons.

For many of us, it is still a big step to a frank and wholehearted acceptance of sexual desire as good, as the grace of a vocation, rather than something shameful and dirty. For others, that step is possible, but is soon hedged with qualifications—sexual desire is not dirty, maybe, but it is selfish. It is a drive for pleasure without responsibility, or an urge for satisfaction of selfish desires. And what is selfish is even worse than what is dirty—selfishness is our root sin. In this view, sex has somehow to be purified or sublimated before it can be sacramental.

Our experience, though, which we ought to trust, teaches us otherwise. People are at their best, their most unselfish, when they are in love and feeling a high level of sexual awareness of, and desire for, each other. Falling in love is really a conspiracy between God and chemistry that fits St. Augustine's famous description of grace as something "done in us without us." The attraction between a particular man and woman is inexplicable in any natural terms; other people wonder what they see in each other, while they, in turn, wonder why everyone else doesn't see what they see. And the attraction is deep within—it shakes people to their roots, overturns perceptions of what is real and what is unreal, alternately chills and heats, reverses our natural fascination with ourselves into a total preoccupation with another. And it is certainly done without us— we do not, and cannot, choose to make it happen; it results from a series of seeming coincidences which need not have happened at all. And yet, when it does happen, it seems so obviously right and true that we can only attribute it to some power beyond us, who knows better than we what is good for us. Sexual attraction is the grace of a vocation.

This ecstasy is the beginning of a call to sacramental sexuality, to genital sexuality, which expresses and brings grace, which lasts a lifetime, and has its own definite pattern of growth. In that process of growth, spouses gradually come to a deeper and deeper intimacy in which they paradoxically—and to their great surprise—find that in putting another's fulfillment ahead of their own, they mysteriously find their own. When we abandon our concern to preserve our separate identity, we instead find that identity enhanced; in entrusting our happiness to the hands of another, we receive it back more fully than if we had nervously clutched it to ourselves. In the sacrament of matrimony, we discover that in losing our life, we find it, in and with our spouse.

Genesis 2:18 notes that in God's view, "It is not good for the man to be alone." What we understand in these words, however, is not a solution to the problem of loneliness. There are many married persons who are lonely, and many unmarried persons who are not. We see, rather, a transcending of the exclusive boundaries of the self, a decentering through sexual intimacy, which opens us to new reality through another person. This new reality is the process of marital intimacy, the process of repeatedly answering the call of sexual desire, leading to the ecstatic abandonment of self to another that brings fulfillment of the self in communion. For Catholics, that fulfillment has a whole added dimension—it is communion with Father, Son and Spirit. It is eternal life. It is what Jesus prayed for at the Last Supper: "I pray not only for these, but for those also who through their words will believe in me. May they all be one. Father, may they be one in us, as you are in me and I am in you, so that the world may believe it was you who sent me. I have given them the glory you gave to me, that they may be one as we are one. With me in them and you in me, may they be so completely one that the world will realize that it was you who sent me and that I have loved them as much as you loved me" (John 17:20–23).

CHAPTER II

MAINTAINING
SEXUAL INTIMACY

A pattern, or cycle, in which romance fades is common in marriages—so common, in fact, that couples often marry with the expectation that it will happen. Or at least, when a young couple in the full enthusiasm of first love marry with the idea that theirs, at least, will last forever, the unspoken expectations of the older married people who know them are more cynical. And those who do marry with a hope for something better often see the same cycle happening to them and resign themselves to it, assuming that it is inevitable. They may become quietly cynical, or openly discouraged; they may give up hope. Some find the courage to renew their romance, under the impetus of sexual desire. But they, too, may find the cycle repeating itself—from falling in love, to settling down, to bottoming out, to beginning again—only to settle down and bottom out again (Anzia and Durkin, pp. 15–70).

Why does this pattern occur so often? If sexual passion is a sacramental cause of grace, a divinely powerful instrument for healing selfishness, why is it not more effective? Why does sexual desire decline? The question is not a matter of will power, for many spouses have tried their best to avoid that decline. They try to be more attentive to each other, to spend more time together, to develop common interests. But even then an atmosphere seems to slowly develop so that their life becomes dull, with a few interludes of joyous intimacy. They live in an emotional desert that has an occasional sexual oasis. Their relationship becomes a companionate one.

Their usual conversation, on the telephone or at the dinner table, becomes somehow different from what it was when they were dating. In fact, we can often go into a restaurant and tell, just by looking at them, which couples are married and which are not. The long-married ones are sedate and mildly bored, with no sexual spark between them, while the not-yet-married show an obvious enthusiasm for each other as they communicate through a sexual prism. They are not just interested in where they are, or what is going on around them, or even what they are saying to each other. They are intensely alert to, absorbed in, each other as special persons.

Often, though, couples eventually come to look on their sexual urgency for each other as history, a thing of the past. They appreciate it for what it was then, a force that brought them together in the first place and gave them a good start. But later life becomes earnest, responsible, plodding. They have occasional verdant spots, full of the old play and joy, and then return to the desert of duty. When they think of each other during the day, they think of a partner, an agreeable companion, or someone they owe something to—but not as sexual lovers. They lose the sexual urgency that constitutes their basic identities as husband and wife; they come to be "just" friends. They live together peaceably enough, and meet their responsibilities. But they have lost the sexual passion that is the core of the sacrament of matrimony. Their life together is no longer marked by the ecstatic self-abandon of sexual lovers.

We are not referring now to frequency of intercourse. Many couples in the cycle of settling down have satisfying sexual activity, and have it often enough. But sacramental sexuality is a union of total persons, not just genital organs. We are referring to the loss of an atmosphere, of a total awareness of each other as sexually desired and loved. The loss of this kind of awareness of each other as a daily constant is like color blindness, or the loss of a sense organ. The relationship is not destroyed; but an important, even basic, aspect of it is lost. Sex becomes an event instead of an aura, something the spouses do together rather than the context in which they do everything. The two face outward instead of toward each other—perhaps even in a physical way. Many couples will be in the same room, even having a conversation, without meeting each other's eyes. But people with sexual passion as the context of their life together are always looking at each other, at least inwardly, even when they are physically apart. They are the center of each other's attention no matter where they are and what they are doing.

Many outwardly, ceremonially, married people, then, are not really, not interiorly, married. They haven't acquired the new identity that marriage brings, but have, to all intents and purposes, remained single. In the externals of living together and enjoying sexual intercourse, they may have changed; they share expenses and do things together—including having and raising children. But in the depths of their minds and hearts—in how they view the world, themselves, and each other—they have remained single. They do not see themselves and each other as basically, primarily, and constantly, tied together by the bond of sexual desire. Their sexual love is not the focus of their perceptions of themselves. They may feel important to each other, may make willing sacrifices for each other. But their life—even though it is a common life—becomes fragmented, divided into separate compartments. And their marriage is only one of those compartments.

In a true marriage, however, a woman never thinks of herself as this individual, private person. She sees herself, always and only, as her husband's beloved. But she cannot see herself that way unless she deliberately and constantly cultivates her maximum sexual desire for her husband, her desire to be totally and ecstatically abandoned to him. To be a wife is not primarily to be loved and cared for, to have one's needs and desires taken care of. It is not to be demanding and possessive, to have a private identity that her husband caters to. It is to be utterly and joyously given over to her husband. And that kind of self-abandon is simply not possible without a continuously cultivated sexual passion. Similarly, a true husband does not think of himself as primarily a lawyer, a doctor, or a bus driver. He is primarily, and constantly, the beloved of his wife, the lover who makes her the complete center of his attention. He belongs to her, and not to himself. He is tied to her—not by duty, or moral uprightness, and certainly not by her dominance and control—but by his promise to be hers. And that promise cannot be kept if sexual passion dies.

The decline of passion, then, is a violation of a couple's marriage vows, a genuine infidelity even if neither has sexual relations with another person (Greeley, *Sexual Intimacy*, pp. 171–189). The fading of romance is the marring and obscuring of a sacramental symbol. For in their vows, the two had promised to be sexually present to each other all the days of their lives. They promised to belong no longer to themselves, but to each other. But without strong and continuing sexual passion, a husband can easily be his own man, even while taking very good care of his wife. He can care for her out of a sense of duty rather than sheer enthusiasm for her as a person. Without strong and continuing sexual passion, a wife becomes very much her own woman—devoted to making a comfortable home, perhaps, taking care of all her husband's lesser needs. But without the desire that keeps him as her beloved at the center of her attention and her motivation, she is still living as an unmarried woman.

Sexual desire takes us out of such self-containment, such self-primacy. Thus sexual passion, instead of being one segment or compartment of a marriage, must be the total aura and context of the life of spouses. Sexual love is not just one of the things that they occasionally do together, like eating and making decisions about their children. Everything they do, together and apart, should come out of, and be colored by, their sexual desire for each other. Wouldn't we agree that a dating couple who felt no spark of sexual attraction for each other were a poor prospect for marriage? No matter how good two persons might be, and how good to each other, the absence of sexual passion is too strong a deficiency to overlook. But it is just as serious a defect ten years after the wedding, or twenty, or fifty, as six months before.

But many married people do gradually sink into just that decline of passion. As with the color blind, who can see well enough but perceive everything as gray, spouses with inhibited or suppressed sexual passion find their daily life gray. They function well enough in society and with each other, but miss out on the full joy and beauty that are there for those who can see. Some, of course, fall in love with someone else in order to fill their emptiness. Others fall in love with their work instead, or a hobby. But the real tragedy is seeing themselves as private persons.

That self-primacy mars and obscures the symbolism of their life together because it directly contradicts the generous, altruistic love that a sacrament is meant both to symbolize and cause. The marred symbolism, in turn, inhibits the power of the sacrament to cause the divine life that saves us from sin and death. And that weakening reduces the ability of spouses to love each other as Jesus loves us all. Thus inhibited passion leads to inhibited intimacy, not only with each other but with the three divine Persons who live in us, and in whom we live, when we love. And inhibited intimacy soon feeds the decline of passion. The cultivation of sexual passion in marriage is thus quite literally a matter of life and death, of eternal life and eternal death.

Let us try to understand this inhibition of sexual passion more clearly, for we are not speaking just of something emotional, that makes people feel less good than they might otherwise. Orgasm is pleasurable, and sexual frustration is not. But emotional comfort is not the main point at issue, not even the generalized pleasure in being alive that people feel as a result of regular, satisfying sexual intercourse. We are speaking of something deeper, the basic orientation of a person's life—what he or she sees as the center of the universe, as more important than anything else. Sexual passion, we are arguing, can be—and in a sacramental marriage, must be—a powerful force for decentering people from themselves. And that decentering is the essence of the love that is the spiritual life of Catholics.

Thus the deeper result of inhibiting sexual passion, of allowing romance to fade in a marriage, is that the spouses do not experience that decentering. They remain self-centered, ungenerous, alienated, unloving, excluded from intimacy with anyone, including the triune God. The decline of sexual passion allows other activities to take first place instead of one's beloved spouse. In a crisis, perhaps, where such a husband had to choose between, say, his wife and his job, he would choose his wife. But in his daily life, she would not have the same importance that she once had. She would be merely one segment of his life, not the basis of the whole. Rather than being an absolute priority, she would be one interest among many. He would frequently expect her to "understand," to postpone her needs for the sake of one of his other interests. In such a decline of giving first priority to each other, spouses often find their sexual desire becoming intermittent. And an atmosphere of boredom and ennui slowly develops.

We are quick to think of excuses for this decline of passion. We find faults in each other that we were not aware of before we began to live together—her conversation is often shallow, his interests are narrow. But shallow conversation and narrow interests were no barrier to sexual desire when we fell in love. Maybe we blame our early training for making us sexually inhibited. But that training was overcome once, when we fell in love.

The added responsibilities of married life are sometimes cited as an excuse for the neglect of passion. But it we think about it, we can see that each stage of life has a full measure of responsibilities. The ones we had when we first fell in love did not inhibit our sexual feelings. "Being too busy" is never a valid excuse for anything, for the fact is that each of us has the very same amount of time—twenty-four hours every day. Thus, if I think I do not have time to do something, I really do have that time, but choose to spend it on something else. If I am too busy to find time for cultivating my sexual desire for my spouse, that is only because I am choosing to spend my time at something else—I am giving something else priority over the ecstatic self-abandon that I promised in my wedding vows.

Sometimes people cite natural sexual differences as the reason why they grow apart. Men and women are bound to go in different directions because they have different ways of seeing the world and setting up their priorities. Thus, it is only natural for a man to become preoccupied with his work and for a woman to become absorbed in housework and children. But spouses are no more male and female than they were at the beginning of their romance, when sexual differences drew them together rather than edging them away from each other.

And behind all of these excuses is the tendency to blame the other partner instead of taking responsibility for our own feelings. "If only she took better care of herself," he might say, "then I would be more sexually excited by her." "If only he would pay more attention to me," she might tell herself, "I would really be turned on to him." But when they were dating, she wasn't dependent on his attention. She could listen to him all day, hanging on his every word. He was so fascinated by her that they could spend the whole day together, totally mesmerized, and then talk on the telephone ten minutes after they parted. They didn't look to their beloved partners to turn them on—they had a natural sexual responsiveness welling up from within, and they constantly sought ways to foster it.

What is really at work behind the decline of sexual passion in marriages is the innate human fear of intimacy, especially of sexual intimacy. The self-abandon of orgasm is thrilling at first, one of the most intense pleasures we can feel. So is the self-abandoning fascination with another person that leads to endless hours of conversation. But intimacy has its own inner law—it must either grow or die. And when it comes time for intimacy to grow, we easily become frightened. It is threatening to allow ourselves into a situation of self-abandon—where we cannot be our own man or woman. The problem is not in the other person, or in our upbringing, or in external circumstances. It is in ourselves—in the deep longing of every human· heart to keep itself for itself. We cannot quite believe that intimacy is a unity-with-distinctness. We fear that it is simply unity, that in giving our life over to another we will lose it.

In fact, we have a double fear that makes us hold back from intimacy for two opposite reasons. We are afraid, on the one hand, of being possessed and controlled, afraid that if we get too close to someone we will lose our independence and, ultimately, our cherished identity as the unique person that each of us is. One of our children expressed this fear very clearly recently; "Mama," she said, "Amanda thinks that just because I am her friend, she owns me." "Oh?" said the mother, "what do you mean?" The child replied, "She thinks she can tell me who else to play with and who not to play with." That is exactly a fear that we carry with us all our lives—a fear that urges us to "stay cool," to "hang loose," not to get too closely involved with people because if we do, we will come under their control. We won't have control of our own lives, our own selves anymore.

But if we understand love and intimacy correctly, especially in their perfect model in the triune God, whose perfect love is the grace by which we love, we need have no such fear. To love is to wish to another person what is good for that person's sake. Thus someone who truly loves us is not going to control or possess us, but will encourage our individuality and independence, because that is good for us. St. Thomas gives a simple, but very illuminating example: if a singer truly loves a writer, and wishes a close intimacy with him, that love is not a desire for the writer to become a singer like his lover, thus giving up his unique identity as a writer. Rather, the singer will want and encourage and work for the writer's development and success as a writer, and enjoy that success as his own when it comes about.

This feature of love is startlingly clear in the Trinity, where three persons, who are more fully persons than we are, enjoy a unity that is more perfect than any other. And yet, in that perfect unity, their three distinct identities are not weakened or threatened, but rather established. The Father is more Father, not less so, in his love for the Son; and the Son finds his identity as Son, not Father, established rather than weakened by the Father's loving closeness to him.

Our other fear of intimacy, the other side of the coin of control and possession, is our fear that if we do preserve our independence and uniqueness, we will be alone, isolated, uncared for. We have a profound feeling that it does no good to be a special person, to have a unique identity, if no one knows and no one cares about it. We fear that if we do develop our own interests and talents, we will become more and more differentiated from other people and, in the process, more and more separated from them. Thus we tend to inhibit our real identity, to adjust and cover it up, in order to be accepted.

But again, if we understand love and intimacy correctly, especially in their perfect model in the Trinity, there is no place at all for such a destructive self-surrender. For to love people is not to grovel and conform, to give up our own well-being in order to promote theirs. To love is to put myself at their service, true, to seek their good as my own, to decenter my attention and energies from my own isolated welfare to my true fulfillment in communion with them. But to devote myself to the well-being of others, to put myself into communion with them, requires that I have a self to give. The ability to love requires a strong self-esteem, and that self-esteem must be solidly grounded in reality.

Thus, precisely as a loving service to others, I will seek the maximum development of my unique self, and will cherish and value that development as a distinct good in its own right. To return to St. Thomas's example, if I am a singer and wish to find fulfillment in communion with a writer, I will not seek to become a writer myself, thus defeating my own identity, sacrificing it to the writer. I will, instead, see that my writer friend needs, for his own fulfillment as a writer, my maximum development as a singer. He needs communion with me—not with a masochistic clone of himself, but precisely with a person, one who is free, autonomous, self-confident, with my own unique identity.

Where, then, is the communion that heals loneliness, if writer and singer become, with each other's encouragement and help, more and more differentiated from each other? Won't they grow apart as they go their separate ways? The answer is, no—not if they truly love each other. For in so loving, and supporting each other's unique identities, they identify with each other's identities. And that identification brings them into communion. The singer's singing success becomes a fulfillment for the writer because the writer has chosen to make it his own; the same is true for the writer's writing success as a fulfillment for the singer. The two do not live separate, parallel lives that never meet. For they share the individuated selves that they become.

Here, again, an understanding of divine intimacy can help us. There are no more highly differentiated persons than the three Persons in one God—the Father is no one's son and never will be, and neither of the other Persons will ever be Father. The uniqueness of their three identities is greater than we can imagine. And yet their unity, as they share those identities in perfect mutual understanding and love, is also greater than we can imagine.

We are to go forth and do likewise. We are afraid of intimacy, because in our lives intimacy is flawed and imperfect. We find our autonomy threatened by closeness, and our closeness threatened by autonomy, but not because that is the nature of intimacy. Rather, we find these evils, and fear them, because our intimacy is never perfect. We can reject each other and possess each other, as the divine Persons cannot. But when we do, we are violating intimacy, not establishing it. We can fall into a selfish refusal of transcendence, as the divine Persons cannot. We can fail to share our different selves, as the divine Persons cannot. We can use and abuse, ignore and damage each other, in a thousand ways, that are impossible to the three Persons in one God. But when we do, these sufferings, and our fear of them, are not due to the nature of intimacy. They are due to failures in intimacy. And those failures can be overcome in intimacy itself, in the decentered, altruistic love that brings intimacy about.

Truly we have nothing to fear from intimacy. We have nothing to fear except the fear of intimacy itself. For the nature of intimacy, and of the love which alone brings it about, is a paradox. But the paradox, though hard to realize, is perfectly true: our uniqueness and independence are not opposed to our unity and closeness with each other. For love is, precisely, making our own the uniqueness of the one we love. Thus, the more we love each other, the more unique and free we will want each other to be. And in that very wanting, we will become one with each other. For the good of another that I foster because I take it to be my own, is my own—by that very fact. Intimacy is unity-in-distinctness. These two features are not opposed, but actually enhance each other.

This same fear of intimacy, and the same cure for it in intimacy, are the key to promoting continuous sexual passion in a marriage. When we are sexually aware and desirous of a beloved spouse, we simply are not our own person. We no longer belong to ourselves. And such a loss of our private self is frightening. Independence and privacy are overthrown by sexual passion. Sexual desire decenters our attention and concern from ourselves. Orgasm is a great pleasure, but putting ourselves into the hands of another person may not be. We may not fear that our spouse will be terribly domineering or possessive. But we do dislike, in the deep perversity of the human heart, the very idea of making someone else—anyone else—as important as ourselves. We resist giving up our self-primacy.

The conflict, then, between maintaining sexual desire and allowing it to atrophy is basically a conflict between egoism and altruism, between self-importance and self-abandon, between selfishness and love. And that conflict is precisely the basic proclamation of the Gospel: our spiritual life, a life of intimacy with Father, Son and Spirit, is basically a death to our self-primacy, a losing of our life in order to find it. Sexual love is a death and a resurrection—a death to our single, private selves, and a resurrection to new life in our coupled selves. And that dying and rising is precisely the sacramental power of matrimony. Sexual desire is a powerful interior impulse, the grace of a vocation to be other-centered rather than self-centered.

Thus, when couples allow their sexual desire to fade, they are weakening a very powerful instrument of salvation. Marital spirituality, then, indeed, married life, is sexual. It is not a way of life that includes sex. It is a sexual way of life. When sexual feeling between a couple is high, their awareness of and alertness to each other is also high—they don't fail to notice each other because they are preoccupied with some other interest. Their level of responsiveness to each other is also high, as is their general satisfaction and joy in living. That joyful intimacy is their vocation, God's plan for them. It is the occasion, indeed the instrument, of their closeness to God. The devils of selfishness—vengeful anger, self-pity, meanness of spirit, vindictiveness, possessiveness—take their flight.

Of course we are not speaking of sexual intercourse, as we said earlier, for that is only one expression of sexual love. Rather, the sacramental life of a couple creates a sexual aura in their home and their entire lives. They are no longer to live, no longer to be, as they were before their wedding vows. Nor are they to perceive themselves, nor be perceived, as they once were. A married person's spouse is never irrelevant to what that person is doing. A sexual way of life means that the spouses never become irrelevant to each other, even for a moment. Whether physically in each other's presence or not, they are to be in each other's minds and hearts, by a passionate sexual awareness and desire.

When couples achieve such continuous sexual intimacy, their persons are transformed. They are more willing to forgive—not just each other, but everyone else they meet. They are, in every contact with another person, less touchy, less sensitive, less fickle. They are more gentle with children, more relaxed in letting them blossom and grow. They are less infected with the consumerism that is the mark of our culture—the effort of people to fill with material things the emptiness left in the wake of declining sexual passion. All of these attitudes are gospel virtues, the marks of those who love each other as Jesus loved us. Sexual desire is not just a great psychological force. In the sacrament of matrimony, its power is transformed. It is a healing, redemptive, God-given grace.

And our God is a generous God. He doesn't give the grace of sexual love just for a time, or just to a chosen few. Lifelong, all-pervasive sexual desire is possible to spouses of all physical conditions and every age, in marriages long or short, between people of varying levels of education and wealth, of infinitely varied personalities. Passion need not fade with time. It is not an interference with our spiritual life, nor a distraction from the love of God. It is one of his ways of saving us from ourselves, of bringing us into deeper intimacy with him. It is the way in which most people live out the gospel message of death to self.

St. Paul put it clearly: "Husbands, your bodies are not your own; wives, your bodies are not your own." (1 Cor. 7:4) In the Bible, the term *body* refers not just to a person's physical part, but to his whole self, mind and heart as well as body. Paul recommends, then, that our very selves are no longer our own, for we belong totally to each other. A husband is to treat his wife as himself, and *vice versa*. But such identification, such seeking the good of another as our own, becomes easy and spontaneous in the warmth of continuously fostered sexual passion.

Couples who make the effort to be sexually aware and desirous of each other become truly married persons, not just persons who once got married. Whether together or alone, making love, playing baseball with their kids, or taking part in the liturgy, they are truly responsive to each other as persons. They are not preoccupied with past, unforgiven hurts, nor fearful of future demands from each other. Nothing distracts them from each other. Over the years, the lines of separation between them become fainter and fainter. They take each other on, in an intimacy which is neither threatening nor difficult. They become a credible symbol of the intimacy in God's own life, of the love that God would pour forth in all our hearts.

But the possibility of such intimacy is practically nil without the deliberate cultivation of sexual passion. Hence we are truly proposing a new specific form of spirituality in the Church. We have not yet gone far enough in correcting our attitudes toward sexuality if we say, "Well, all right, sex is not evil, maybe, but at best it is a mere human reality. And Christians are called to higher things. Sexual desire is all right in its place, but couples find their salvation in other ways—in prayer, self-sacrifice, frequent confession and attendance at mass."

Sexual passion is the center, the basis, of the spiritual life of married people. A couple who make the most of their sexual desire are the clearest symbol we know of the Trinity. For the three divine Persons do not live a life of ministry to each other's needs, or a life of sharing common tasks. They live a life of complete giving and receiving of each other's very selves. Under the power of sexual desire, married couples reach a similar intimacy. True, spouses do have to meet each other's needs and share common tasks and activities, for human persons, being imperfect persons, do have needs and activities. But such ministry to each other, and such sharing, are not what married life is mainly about. Mainly, being married is belonging to each other, exchanging personal selves in loving intimacy, becoming bone of each other's bone and flesh of each other's flesh.

Something very powerful is needed for such intimacy, some force that can overcome our deep tendency to keep ourselves for ourselves, to remain private, single persons rather than enter into wedded intimacy. And that something is provided by God's providence. It is grace, of course, but grace that comes through an especially appropriate human instrument: sexual desire, sexual awareness as a constant state of mind. When such desire is cool, spouses can be objective and dispassionate about each other. They can be restrained and balanced in their dealings with each other. One or the other can easily say "Well, she's wrong about this, I'll just have to go ahead anyway in order to get things done." Such balancing of marital union with other values, such a reasoned calculation, is not possible to those who maintain the sexual desire that first drew them together.

People who are in love are crazy about each other; their dealings with each other, their decisions in all areas of their lives, do not follow a reasoned and predictable calculation. They belong to each other, not to themselves, so deeply that they always put each other first, always take each other's side. Such unity of persons is obvious to all who know them. Such couples are the clearest and most credible symbols we can think of of the ecstatic intimacy of persons that is the inner life of God.

What is at stake, then, in the deliberate cultivation of sexual desire, sexual awareness, and sexual intimacy is not just a shallow pleasure, or even the prevention of divorce. Married life indeed is a specific kind of spirituality, just as the Jesuits, the Dominicans, the Franciscans and the Carmelites have distinctive spiritualities. Jesuits wouldn't be Jesuits without the discernment of spirits. They might be pious, good, holy, prayerful men—but they would lack the distinctive mark of Jesuit spirituality.

Something similar is true of sacramental married couples. The distinctive mark of marital spirituality is sexual intimacy. A couple who lack that might be good persons, self-sacrificing, kind, regular in their religious practices. But without a deep and abiding sexual intimacy, they would lack the distinctive mark of their kind of spirituality. We cannot, simply cannot, downgrade the importance of sexual affection. It is not evil, of course; but neither is it "merely" natural or human, something we should bypass in order to come into union with God. Sexual love is a sacrament, an instrument of divine grace. We neglect it at the peril of our salvation. Catholic spiritual life is incarnate—all spiritualities, celibate and married. But the spirituality of marriage, rooted as it is in the sense of touch, is the most clearly incarnate of all. And that carnality is meant to be a model, a sacrament, of the trinitarian intimacy that saves us.

Some will say that such a cultivation of sexual passion is unrealistic, that spouses cannot be excited about each other, enthusiastic about each other, twenty-four hours a day. There is work to be done, after all. That view is precisely what we are challenging. Spouses not only can, but must, live in an aura of sexual desire for each other. That is their vocation, the heart of the marital symbol. That aura is possible—it exists among the engaged; it can be maintained.

Such a view, which is truly a spirituality of marriage, is certainly counter-cultural. Many of our secular contemporaries believe that marriage kills passion, that it is better to live together without being married, that if a couple does marry, the rest of their life together is downhill as far as passion is concerned. We hold, instead, that wedding vows are a most solemn promise to cultivate sexual desire, and to make that cultivation the first priority of daily life.

It is easy to imagine what such a continuously maintained sexual aura would do for children. People go to great lengths to do what is right for their children—seek advice, make sacrifices, talk things through. Actually, the best thing any couple can do for their children is to maintain their sexual awareness of, and desire for, each other. When such tender, generous, and passionate intimacy is evident to children, they experience their own roots in a deeply comfortable, and deeply comforting, way. They also see their own future set before them in a hopeful manner. They come to believe—in fact, breathe such belief as an atmosphere—that, yes, love is real, and will last, and can be trusted. A home filled with sexual desire has a gentle, nonpunitive, nonvindictive aura about it. Such a home seldom sees vindictive anger. The people in it see, and praise, the best in each other.

Of all the resources that a couple accumulate over the years—house, job, bank account, even children—the most important is their own God-given gift of sexual desire. Gratitude for that gift was expressed beautifully by one husband we know of. At his thirty-fifth wedding anniversary party, with children and grandchildren gathered around him, in a beautiful home that was a sign of his hard work for the family's financial security, the man's wife proposed a toast. "To the man," she said, "who made all of this possible." He immediately held his glass up and proposed an answering toast. "To the woman" he grinned, "who made all of this necessary."

The atmosphere of a Catholic home, then, should send a loud and clear message to those who live in it, and to those who visit, namely, that it is all right to let yourself go, to let go of yourself, in a community of intimates. Such an atmosphere will give living, breathing evidence that an almost incredible joy awaits anyone who has the courage to die to his private self only to rise to new life, to a new and better self, in ecstatic communion with a lover. That is precisely the gospel message, and we are now at the root of the dynamic by which the sacrament of matrimony builds the Church. We shall look at that dynamic at length later on. But for now, let us look at the implications for Catholic pastors, confessors, and marriage counselors and therapists.

For anyone advising and guiding couples, the overriding question is not how kind they are to each other, how many favors they do for each other, how many common projects they share. The main question is their level of sexual desire: "On an average day, say, at two o'clock on a Thursday afternoon, how sexually aware of your wife are you? How desirous are you of your husband?" We don't mean fantasies of intercourse, or plans for it, though such mental images may well be part of this sexual aura. We are thinking, instead, of how spouses perceive their identities, and how that perception motivates their choices, day in and day out.

The question is, also, how they perceive each other—as just friends, albeit special ones, like brother and sister, or as the passionately loved centers of each one's life. No matter how generous, self-sacrificing and patient spouses may be with each other, no matter how close in shared secrets and common interests, without the sexual aura, their life is simply not marital. And that lack of the distinctively marital quality is no small failure. It is the absence of the causal symbol, and symbolic cause, of the intimacy with the Trinity that is their salvation. That intimacy is what gives value and power to their patience, their generosity, their shared interests. It is their union with God. And to miss out on that is to miss out on eternal life, to remain in that sin whose wages is death.

Advisors of married people, then, have to help couples to maintain their sexual desire for each other, help them to foster and cherish the passion that first brought them together. It will help us to understand that kind of guidance if we take a brief look at the work of marital and family therapists, those who seek to heal marriages and families in which something has gone wrong. The profession of therapy has, of course, grown out of modern psychology, which has, quite independently of the Church, discovered the importance of intimacy for mental and emotional health. The people working in that profession have also discovered many of the laws and techniques by which intimacy can grow. They have also described well and clearly some of the common obstacles to marital intimacy, and learned ways for overcoming those obstacles.

Indeed, the problems that therapists work with are, more often than not, just exaggerated, extreme instances of problems that all couples face to some degree in their ordinary life. Furthermore, since intimacy—with each other and with our triune God—is the core and essence of Catholic spirituality—modern psychological discoveries about intimacy can be joined with the basic principles of Catholic marital spirituality to give us the basis for spiritual guidance for Catholic couples. The main focus of marital therapy, as of the life of couples who do not need therapy, is communication—the various ways in which people give outward expression to their inward thoughts and feelings so as to share these with each other.

The techniques of communication, then, are the techniques of intimacy. For intimacy is the sharing of selves (in a loving way), and we are not pure spirits who simply see into each other's selves. Our persons are somewhat hidden and have to be revealed through material means of communication—speech, writing, gestures, physical actions. The language *par excellence* of sexual intimacy is, of course, sexual intercourse, the epitome of body language. But words are important, too. Marital therapists can tell us some important elements of verbal communication as a way to marital intimacy.

The patterns of good communication—the kind that fosters true intimacy—were noticed some twenty years ago by Pope John Paul II, when he was bishop of Crakow, Poland. The book in which these structures are described has now been translated into English, with the title *Love and Responsibility*. There the Holy Father offers a paradigm, which we shall set forth and then illustrate in an actual case. In the words of Bishop Wojtyla, "Love in the individual develops by way of attraction, desire and goodwill. Love however finds its full realization not in an individual subject, but in a relationship between subjects, between persons" (Wojtyla, p. 95). Three elements are mentioned here: attraction, desire, and goodwill. When we have the good fortune to meet a couple who live these values in their whole relationship, what do we notice?

First, they are attracted, or drawn to, each other rather than to anything or anyone else around them. They have each other's attention. They look at each other with—in Ring Lardner's famous phrase—"a look you could pour on a waffle." Their looking is slow, relaxed, lingering over personal details and contours. The way they use their eyes is like a kind of touching, allowing thousands of little details of shape, texture, and color, as well as the minute-by-minute changes, to impact on their minds and hearts. They use the poet's way of looking—a mode of perception that comes easily to engaged couples, very special friends who are ready to marry. Such looks are quite different from the wary scrutiny of people who are reacting rather than responding, searching for possible attacks or evasions. The pupils of lovers dilate in pleasure, not fear.

The attraction is pleasurable, too. They allow themselves to take in each other's personal beauty in a way that relaxes their bodies. They turn toward each other and modulate their movements in gentle harmony, like skillful dancers. Their posture brings them face to face and they accommodate to each other, at times imitating each other's gestures like mirror images. Their hands and arms open out, unlike a hostile couple who use their limbs to block sight of each other, or turn away with arms folded to minimize sensual contact.

They listen to each other, savoring, appreciating, even caressing each other's voices. The way a message is formed becomes as important as what is said, and a pathway into the other person's self. What is he or she telling me through tone of voice, pitch, rapidity of speech, choice of words? How can I put the other person's experience into my own words, to express what I am understanding of his or her life? They struggle with such questions and strive to enter each other's worlds. In doing so they learn to resonate with each other, like tuning forks in sympathetic vibration which, though separate, sound the same tone.

The second element of their love is the reason for such attentiveness: their desire for each other's very persons. They see each other as good, not just in some abstract way, but as good for themselves, here and now, in the concrete reality of the present moment. They reach out to each other, seeking closeness, wanting to be together. Each yearns to taste the other—a yearning symbolized so well by a kiss. A kiss obviously says, "Become a part of me; let me partake of you, as I do the food I eat, which maintains my very life." Their craving to become one with each other as persons, felt as a desire to merge physically, culminates in sexual desire. In this desire, spouses open themselves to the most intimate union possible this side of the grave, the wish to enter into each other's bodies. They long as well to mingle themselves in a fruitful way, having children as a way of increasing their very selves. In Shakespeare's words,

> From fairest creatures we desire increase,
> That thereby beauty's rose might never die.
> (Sonnet I)

Increasing ourselves through children is a way of seeking to make immortal the selves that we love in each other.

Attraction and desire merge with the third element of love mentioned in Bishop Wojtyla's description—goodwill, altruism, or benevolence—a warm friendliness toward each other, by which lovers seek not each other's harm and destruction, but each other's well-being. The warmth of their goodwill is evident in many ways: sometimes actual bodily warmth, felt in a lover's embrace; or the tone of voice that conveys the message "You're not alone now, for I'm with you, walking the road by your side." Such warmth comes from the life within each lover, given as gift to the other, a passionate, heartfelt gift of each other's very self.

Warmth of goodwill is not, however, a sentimental niceness which glosses over the conflicts that are unavoidable. Conflicts are a part of love simply because people differ from each other and change as time goes on. Sometimes altruistic love takes the form of a confrontation, a loving statement of disagreement, of hurt, or of displeasure. Here the warmth may gain the intensity of fire—as we say, sparks may fly. But the fire is not that of vengeful anger, of an assaultive resentment, or a desire to hurt or retaliate.

Here we need to see the difference between two different ways of speaking to each other, the reactive and the responsive. The first destroys intimacy, while the second builds it. The destructive, reactive way comes from fear and aims at protectively concealing a person's self. But responsive talking comes from love, from an altruistic and trusting desire to reveal oneself. Let us see in an example how a confrontation differs from an attack, and—even though it expresses conflict and displeasure—is a desire for better understanding and deeper intimacy. An angry attack is not such a loving approach; it is a desire to retaliate, to hurt. It puts down and humiliates the person spoken to, thus destroying the equality that is the basis of intimacy. But a confrontation edifies in the root meaning of that term—it builds intimacy. Here is an example:

> *Reactive attack:* "You don't give a damn about me; all you care about is yourself."

> *Responsive confrontation:* "I feel very cut off from you, and I'm upset about that. You seem too preoccupied to even be aware of me and how lonely I feel."

Notice that both statements express a displeasure with the *status quo* and a desire to change it. But the attack implies an accusation and disregards the hurt feelings of the person being blamed. Its impact is punitive and humiliating. The one making the attack is wishing evil, not good, to the other. There is no desire for a loving exchange of selves.

The confrontation, by contrast, does not seek to attack, humiliate, or hurt the other person. It expresses the speaker's current experience of their relationship, in terms of his or her own feelings, in order to improve their exchange of selves. The other person's behavior is described but not criticized, and the description is somewhat tentative or provisional. It does not put the speaker in a know-it-all position of superiority and control. A confrontation allows the other to respond as an equal, revealing his true self, thus deepening their intimacy. It replaces rigid and negative "you" messages with open and tentative and positive "I" messages. An ongoing series of such exchanges can go far to make intimacy deeper.

The message immediately preceding such a confrontation is also important. Those who use a structural approach to family therapy, which makes considerable use of confrontations, employ a technique of using a supportive message as an immediate prelude to a confrontation. Some therapists, with a touch of humor, call this the "stroke-kick" technique, the technique of praising and affirming the other before stating the issue causing displeasure or conflict. The "stroke" communicates, "You *are* worthwhile, and I care about you." This helps the person being confronted to avoid taking the confrontation as an attack. Instead it becomes a message from a person who is *for you, not against you*. The confrontation, thus, is more likely to be accepted in trust, as an expression of love. In the example given, the prelude stroke might be, "You've really done a lot for me, and I appreciate it. But right now I feel very cut off from you, etc." (Cf. S. Minuchin, *Families and Family Therapy*, pp. 226–27.)

Such communication shows how intimates activate their power with each other. They may be quite unequal in power, but out of love they commit themselves to giving up all power struggles, browbeating, one-upmanship and control games. They aim at respectful negotiation, seeing each other as equal in human dignity. They may even sit on chairs of unequal heights, so that their eyes can meet on the same level. Therapists working with reactive couples often have to correct many nonverbal patterns that are incompatible with the equality of intimates, such as one standing above the other, or coming from behind, or literally looking down on the other. The power gap shown by these approaches is incompatible with a loving exchange of selves.

But if people use more appropriate actions, changing their nonverbal behavior, they begin to feel more warm and loving toward each other. Such changes occur naturally when friends reconcile, and this natural process is the basis for techniques used in therapy to help hostile partners in a marriage to become friendly again, to reconcile to a better intimacy. Often the therapist coaches the spouses in techniques or ways of speaking to each other that express the love that is the heart and soul of marital intimacy. The structure described by Bishop Wojtyla, seen in action in marital therapy, thus gives us a pattern of building intimacy throughout the lifetime of a marriage. Marriages that never need therapy follow these same techniques of communication.

Another important element in maintaining the sexual desire that constitutes the sacramental symbol of matrimony is striking the right balance between verbal intimacy and sexual intimacy. Such a balance is not easy, and requires lifelong effort. It is all too easy for couples to use intercourse as a way of avoiding intimacy, to discharge their emotional tensions without ever confronting their differences and problems. But that kind of intercourse is not really intimate, not an exchange of personal selves that can cause and symbolize trinitarian intimacy. On the other hand, it is also easy to use conversation as a way of avoiding sex, postponing intercourse until everything is talked out—including sexual passion. Such conversation is not really intimate, either, because it evades the emotional and bodily exchange that is essential to a communion of selves.

The correct way to maintain sexual intimacy, the sacramental symbol, follows from what we said earlier in this chapter: a constant sexual awareness of, and desire for, each other as the prior condition for conversation. When conflict arises, the way to resolve it is, of course, a conversation that takes the form of a loving confrontation. Without such verbal intimacy, issues remain unresolved and the communion of selves is weak and incomplete. But prior to such confrontations, couples need to be sure that their aura of sexual desire is intact. If it is not, if passion has cooled or turned to repugnance, a time out is called for—not necessarily for intercourse, though that may happen. But at the least a couple should take time to renew their sexual awareness of, and feeling for, each other. With passion burning, they will be together, their problem in front of them for their joint solution. But if ardor is cooled or turned off, if their perception of each other as sexually loved is lost, they are not together. Their problem is between them, and in attacking it, they will be attacking each other.

Catholic psychologists with a keen interest in spirituality have tried, thus, to integrate science with faith, studying clinically the kind of love that is not just healthy, but specifically Christian—in which spouses love each other with the *kenosis,* the self-abandon, with which Jesus loves us. In matrimony, that love becomes sacramental, both symbolizing and causing ecclesial intimacy—the intimacy of an intimacy (the Church) with Intimacy (the Trinity). Sexual intercourse, when it is the heart of a Catholic marriage, is then a nonverbal confrontation *par excellence.* Sexual attacks and power plays, on the other hand, are countersigns. They violate the sacrament, destroy its symbolism, and damage the Church instead of building her up.

But the renewal of a marriage is not a process involving just the two spouses, or even them and an invisible God. This renewal occurs through the people who form Christ's body, through their support and challenges and loving concern. It is through visible people that we encounter the God we cannot see. And this encounter happens on many levels, including the writing and the reading of this very book; for matrimony is founded on the community of faith. It is not a private, or even a coupled, affair. The community, thus, bears a responsibility toward each couple connected to it through the sacrament. All who are the Church, as the people of God and the Body of Christ, need to provide couples with the resources required to enhance the living symbolism of their married life.

There are other practical needs, too. The first is sex education that is complete, accurate, and lifelong. Surely there is no longer any reason to doubt that children and adolescents need much more information, and much fuller communication of positive sexual attitudes and values, than is the usual practice nowadays. Studies have shown that such information does not encourage sexual activity that would not have occurred otherwise. Other studies have shown, though, that a large majority of teenagers—something on the order of 85 percent—find their parents unapproachable on such matters.

It is very important, then, that we do whatever we must to enable parents to become the chief sex educators of their children, by setting an atmosphere at home that enthusiastically appreciates sex as a gift of God. And one main requirement here is sex education for adults throughout the life cycle. We need to understand our own changing sexual needs and possibilities as we mature and age.

A college student told one of the authors of this book of a recent conversation that occurred in his family, in which he, his parents, and his grandparents sat down together and discussed for several hours what sexuality meant to them in their various stages of life. That student was fortunate to have such a family. Such conversations would be beneficial in all families.

Another need—and let's remember that we are speaking here of a sacramental symbol, the most important reality in Catholic spiritual life—is a lifestyle for couples in which time for leisurely, uninterrupted love-making is the item of first priority in their budgeting of time and money. Couples all too easily find, and then settle for, some minimally satisfying way of making love, and then become absorbed in other interests so that sexual skills do not have time to develop. Other concerns become more important, take up time and attention, so that couples may go for days—perhaps weeks and months—without any prolonged time alone together in which their love-making could flourish. Michael Novak, who has written well on Catholic married life, remarked in a recent private conversation that he finds the current popularity of sex manuals somewhat ironic. "The real problem about making love," he said, "is not how, but when—when to find the time."

That *when* is a major problem that every couple must solve if they are to make the most of their love-making, so that intercourse becomes a powerful force for making love, and making love grow. In the first enthusiasm of falling in love, and the heat of youthful passion, we can manage in a few minutes in the back seat of a car. But if we are to become adept, to make that sacramental symbol as full and rich as we can, we must have regular, prolonged uninterrupted time in which to do so. It is not always easy to find a period of an hour or more when both spouses are rested, relaxed in mind and body, and free of possible interruptions. As someone has remarked, there is no faster turnoff than a child's voice in the night. But couples simply have to find such time, plan for it, give it its proper place in the family budget (Greeley, *Sexual Intimacy,* pp. 129–134). If the only way to get it is to hire baby-sitters and go to a motel, then we will do that. If the cost of a weekend away is such that we won't be able to get a new stereo, then we won't get the stereo. Sexual intimacy, sacrament that it is, must have top priority in the spending of our time and money. And such privacy needs official church support. A baby-sitting co-op, in which couples would take turns providing such time off for each other, is an obvious parish project.

Other needs for the development of an accurate sacramental symbol are equally obvious, and we need not go into them in detail. Certainly sex therapy, which is basically an adult form of sex education, can be put to the service of the sacrament of matrimony. We need to be careful, of course, for that burgeoning field has its share of quacks as much as any other. But good therapists can be found, especially those who share the faith, and couples who have sexual problems should be encouraged to seek therapy as a legitimate—and in their case, necessary—response to the grace of their vocation, to the Holy Spirit's call to a deeper marital, which is to say sexual, intimacy. Dioceses could compile lists of approved therapists, those who are not only competent but oriented toward the sacramental nature of sexual intimacy. In fact, Bishop Wojtyla recommended such a use of sex therapy more than twenty years ago (Wojtyla, *Love and Responsibility,* pp. 286–288).

Marriage encounters and marriage enrichment programs, special liturgies for the married, resource centers, support groups, papal statements, bishops' meetings, research by Catholic scholars—all of these, and other practical steps—could be taken to foster the sexual skills of Catholic married couples. Then all of us might see—really see—the sacramental symbolism of marital intimacy. For sexual ecstasy, when it expresses and reveals generous love, is more than a moment of supreme pleasure and psychological closeness. It is more than a legitimized release of tension. It is more than a powerful reassurance through the sense of touch that love is indeed real. It is a symbol of the real presence in us of triune divine love, a symbol that causes what it symbolizes. Christian love-play is a sacrament that draws us into the love-play of the Trinity.

CHAPTER **III**

BARRIERS TO
SEXUAL INTIMACY

In the softly lit room a woman sat, somewhat tense, in a large reclining armchair. She turned her head slightly toward her left shoulder. As she did the gentle lamp light from across the room glistened on her moist eyes.

"We went to the monastery, my husband and I, and it was an upsetting experience for me."

Her lower lip began to quiver ever so slightly as she spoke.

"The abbot had us together in his office," she continued. "And he kept on telling my husband, 'You need to love your wife more. Cherish her! Bring her flowers! That's your problem. You don't love her enough!' John sat there dumb as a log. We took a break, and I refused to return for the next conference. Nothing was happening. It wasn't helping."

She crossed her legs and seemed to lean forward a little. A look of great loss and deep sadness clouded her eyes. "That night," she whispered, "I knew John was very angry at me and didn't want to touch me. As I lay there on the bed, I could hear him washing in the bathroom. The loneliness of that moment was so unbearable that I began to pray that God himself would bend down from heaven and hold me, just hold me closely. I started to cry. John came over to the bed and I sobbed, 'John just hold me, hold me! I need to be held so badly!' And he did. And we lay there close for nearly an hour, until we fell asleep."

62

This couple, both well-educated Catholic lay persons, were struggling with the meaning of intimacy in their lives. In a way similar to many other couples today, both were dissatisfied with their relationship. The wife was piqued at her husband's emotional distance from her; the husband resented her pressuring him for attention. Their everyday communication was typically quite distressed and painful. Clearly they were caught in patterns of ineffective communication. But there was a deeper dimension to their difficulties. They were up against obstructions to an effective marital spirituality.

The relevance of spirituality to everyday distress in marriage, however, is not obvious in our culture. The dominant presupposition in America is that relational problems in marriage are purely "worldly" phenomena. Their improvement requires competent therapy, an objective, matter-of-fact treatment from a professional. This view is a derivative of the positivistic bias of our culture. Running parallel to that popular bias is a dogma tacitly held among professionals, the assumption that "disturbance in human behavior . . . reflects some deficiency within the person or . . . that person's immediate environment" (Urie Bronfenbrenner, *The Ecology of Human Development* p. 290; cf. pp. 258, 289–91); that is, parents, marriage, family. But there is another possibility, namely, that the broader environment—society, Church—may be a crucial factor in an individual person's difficulties. If that be the case, the broader environment might also be a source of healing and strength.

In this view, the broader environment is very important for our spiritual lives, a reality that makes spirituality neither vague nor magical. For the phrase "broader environment" refers to something quite concrete: the consistent patterns of behavior that we can observe in our culture, or in smaller parts of it that constitute subcultures. These patterns are seen in the ways in which people live; they reveal how people comprehend, or think about, life. People's behavior as they move from situation to situation and are affected by situations they don't take part in, is a revelation of their underlying beliefs.

For us Catholics, our spiritual life is a reality that we experience in the subculture known as the Church. In theological language, we are referring to the Church as "fundamental sacrament"—the situation in which we reveal to others our underlying beliefs about life.

The Church is the situation in which we live our spiritual life. Our parish churches are the smaller situations which constitute that larger environment and provide the situations that we actually take part in. But the Church at large is our broader environment, and what happens there can be a source of both marital problems and their healing. Each couple lives in its own situation, just as each person lives in his own family, workplace, and so on. But all are affected by the larger situations in the broader environment—in chanceries and seminaries, in the Vatican—even if they do not participate in them directly. For the broader environment is not separate from the smaller ones—it includes them as its parts. The fundamental sacrament, then, is not married couples, but the Church in which they live their married life. The Church, as the integration of all its members, provides the underlying beliefs according to which they live their various spiritual lives.

In matrimony, one of the common situations, spirituality has as its core the intimate mutuality between the spouses. We would like to deal with this notion of mutuality in terms of the contrast mentioned earlier between reacting and responding. Marital mutuality consists in attaining a high degree of intimate responsiveness with one's spouse, so that at every level of the marital relationship spouses transcend their personal reactiveness. In a way, transcending reactiveness is the basic challenge of living a married life. The challenge can be understood as holding true on a purely natural level. But we can see that the challenge carries over into the supernatural, sacramental dimension of married life. It becomes a mutual ministry of the spouses, which affects, and is affected by, not only their own individual situations, but the interlocking of these into that broader environment, the Church. The Church exists when people respond to each other rather than merely reacting. Let us see how married couples in particular exist in the Church.

Some of the principles and techniques of marital therapy can help us comprehend marital relationships that do not need therapy. And that understanding can help us to understand the sacrament of matrimony and marital spirituality. Marital problems that do require professional therapy are actually extreme or unusually intense forms of difficulties that are common to all marriages. We can even say that such problems *must* be dealt with by couples if their marriages are to be lived in a way that sustains their sacramental mission.

Thus, all spouses, as well as those persons who would seek to give them ordinary spiritual guidance, should be able, not to give professional therapy, but to recognize those problems.

No marriage, indeed, no significant human relationship is problem-free. Imperfect understanding, incomplete acceptance, and half-hearted affirmation bedevil us all in our day by day struggles for meaningful lives together. In a sense, spiritual growth in the sacrament of matrimony *is* a process of ongoing problem solving, for we are not born with the quality of intimacy. Neither do our weddings bestow the gift of intimacy on us instantaneously. We must grow into mutual intimacy gradually and, at times, painfully. In this growth we are up against certain natural barriers to intimacy found in human life itself. They are barriers that mutual love transcends. But that love is possible only if the barriers are recognized: and marital love itself becomes actual only as loving *persons* accept the challenge of confronting those barriers together. In this mutual, cooperative project they become loving *spouses*. Since this process of growing into a loving intimacy happens in marital therapy, a better understanding of the therapeutic process can help us to recognize the prime challenges to intimacy for marriages that are not in therapy.

What are these prime challenges to marital intimacy? Some of the most important ones are the following:

1. an emotional sense of sex as degrading or dangerous;
2. a fear of spontaneity as implying loss of self-worth as a sexual person;
3. a view of the opposite sex as threatening or competitive;
4. a fear of attaining more marital intimacy than one's own parents;
5. desiring one's spouse to function as a parent;
6. protective loyalty toward one's parents; and
7. conflict-avoidance through focusing on some third reality.

These challenges are present to some degree in every marriage. How do they shape experience in marriage? Let's consider each briefly.

An emotional understanding of sex as degrading or dangerous has two main sources. One is biological; the other, cultural. In the former, two intense experiences affect us: eliminative functions and the excitement of sexual arousal. Both appear to deprive us of our security as autonomous persons. Our own excrement shocks the human senses, and the rise of sexual urgency seems to threaten our usual balance. Add to this the many cultural messages that sex is gross, sleazy, and perverse, and we easily become quite ambivalent about our own sexual selves.

First, there is the grossness. One of the most influential of these cultural messages is the misunderstanding of sexuality as purely a matter of instinct. Whether in the guise of the instinct to "preserve the species" or as the residue of our brutal, untamed animality, the upshot is the same. Sexuality is the sleeping giant within us, waiting to surge forth in either benign or malevolent power of instantaneous and gross magnitude. This is *not* true (sexuality is actually a very delicate language, one that must be learned socially and reinforced within a language community), but if we believe it, we will logically follow certain practices. We will strive rigidly to control our sexual impulses, because we fear their strength. We will rebuff our spouse's sexual advances as repulsive and animal. We will slip, by degrees, toward the fallacy that sex is the root of our troubles, a form of gnostic heresy.

From this first point, the grossness of sex, the second follows. The sleaziness of certain sections of our cities—the adult book stores, strip joints, porno houses, and hooker hangouts—convince us that sex itself is unclean. Such a cultural belief is very much like what the object-relations theory of psychotherapy describes as happening with individuals. For example, let's say a woman was raised in a family in which the direct expression of anger was considered wrong and unacceptable. Since it is impossible to live closely with others and avoid irritating experiences, the woman will experience feelings of irritation and anger that she learns not to accept or consciously admit. But the feelings remain a part of her bodily reality even though considered unacceptable. Consequently, she is in conflict with herself whenever she experiences irritation.

To resolve this conflict and escape guilt feelings about these unacceptable experiences, the woman uses a psychological defense called "projective identification." The unacceptable experiences, feelings, desires, and fantasies are attributed to someone else and disowned, so to speak. There has to be someone else around, of course, a person identified as willing to accept this projected ownership, for the defense to work. When there is, however, certain contrasting stereotypes are lived out in tandem. A common example in marriage is the sweet, gentle wife with a raging bull of a husband. The man seems to be angry enough for two people. And he is. He helps his wife avoid the guilt of her anger by adding hers to his own and maintaining the illusion that she never experiences anger. The same thing can happen with sexual excitement. On a large, social scale this projective disowning of sexuality by "respectable" people puts it off onto the sleazy sex merchants. Disreputable feelings "ought" to be owned only by disreputable people.

One of us heard a somewhat humorous example of this tacit devaluation of sexuality once in the conversation of two grade school boys. The younger one in a moment of naive pride exclaimed to his buddy: "You know, my dad has never _____ !" The other one, a European immigrant four years older, responded with a chuckle: "Well then, how did you ever come into the world?" The younger boy immediately did a double take, realizing there must be something wrong with his thinking. There was, but the problem was more than his alone. The connotations of the slang expression for sexual intercourse imply a perverseness, a twisting of reality, which is reinforced by many cultural messages—only "bad' people do that sort of thing. If we were to accept these connotations, we would fall into the dualistic heresies of old such as gnosticism, docetism, and manichaeism. Our spirituality would be based more on the Cartesian dichotomy of mind and matter than on the gospel of the Word made flesh.

But such a devaluation of human bodily existence is still with us. The explicit heresies implied by this distorted spirituality have all been officially condemned, including the philosophical dualism of René Descartes. Yet their influence lingers on, not so much in explicit verbal teaching, but in nonverbal communication and behavior. Whenever we act as if sex were evil, immoral, or dirty and degrading in itself, we communicate, in a language of gesture, the ancient dualistic heresies. We thereby foster the growth of an obstacle to our incarnate spirituality, whether marital or celibate.

Closely related to this negative, destructive model of sex is a fear of *spontaneity*. Some people cannot "let go" enough to experience intimacy. Such a fear of spontaneity is based on anticipation that it will lead to a loss of self-worth as a sexual person. To lose self-worth in this way would mean losing a part of one's identity. Consequently this fear is serious. But it operates somewhat differently in the two sexes. For a man, spontaneity could mean loss of rationality and control. This loss conflicts with a masculine ideal of *always being on top of things.* To spontaneously reach out could be feared as surrendering to a woman, or falling under the sway of her power. Some men will allow themselves to reach out only when they can maintain control, a control expressed as mechanical love-making in their marriages. For such men letting go can even be equivalent to a sin against the self. When coupled with the first obstacle, a notion of sex as sinful, the fear of spontaneity can lead to allowing sexual release only in sordid circumstances. Some men enjoy spontaneity only with prostitutes, because only with such "fallen women" is it felt to be really appropriate. The destructive effect of this "negative spirituality" on marital intimacy is, of course, quite apparent.

For some women spontaneity could mean a loss of feminine dependence and guilt for their aggressiveness. For them reaching out to their husbands in sexual desire smacks of selfishness or even masculinity. They may understand it as a way to seize inappropriate control rather than as a letting go. When such a woman experiences spontaneous desire, she associates it with insecurity. In her view passivity is the really acceptable feminine position. Her esteem must come to her from the outside, especially from some strong male person who accepts her and grants her his approval. The light of self-esteem is reflected by her, rather than radiated from within. Such a belief, however, is a serious flaw in a woman's spiritual life. The Spirit never penetrates to her core, transforming her and enhancing her personal value by enabling her to love ecstatically. It remains on the surface like a thin film. At bottom she believes herself an incomplete, unworthy person, a mere satellite of a greater source.

The third obstacle to intimacy discloses some important background to the first two. Underlying the fears of sex and of spontaneity can be a tacit idea of heterosexual relationships as competitive. According to this model, the opposite sex is considered threatening. Men and women are locked in a sex-based power struggle in which you either win or lose. You must struggle for an advantage or else be taken advantage of by the opposite sex. A significant part of the women's liberation movement stems from this view of inter-sexual relationships as a power struggle.

The spirit of competition, of course, has been a major aspect of American culture for many years. In the past, however, it was restricted to the playing fields and the business districts. Today competition skews marriage on a large scale. Part of this change is due to women's attempt to find an alternative to the satellite model of a woman's role and capacity. The most obvious alternative is to turn the tables, but the ensuing power struggle renders intimacy impossible. Under this rubric a spouse is someone who will use you, not make love. The result becomes a training in vindictiveness. Men become distant, cold, logical critics or obsequious weaklings. Women become either shrews or doormats. Or a calculated cold war develops in which each spouse guards his or her own turf, occasionally detouring into no man's land for a joyless copulation. What a tragic, painful, *folie à deux!*

When couples caught in this destructive dance seek the help of a marital therapist, their situation appears quite formidable. It gives the impression of some baleful adaptation bigger than both of them. Accumulated experience seems to indicate just that, something strong beyond the couple as individuals, as a source of their conflict. Some factor of their broader environment is at work, and the healing of that could heal the couple as well. What might it be? The remaining obstacles to intimacy can give us a glimpse of its contours.

The next four barriers originate in our experiences as children with our parents. One is a fear of attaining more intimacy than they did. As unlikely as this sounds, couples do shrink from outdistancing their parents in achieving intimacy. To do so, it seems, would be to point the finger at the parents as lesser people, as people who didn't "make it." Such an implicit put-down, however, immediately rebounds onto the couple in the form of guilt feelings. The old maxim *misery loves company* has a kernel of truth to it. To outdistance one's parents in intimacy would be to abandon them to their misery. It would risk their anger, rejection, and jealousy. Some people cannot deal with that risk, and so they sabotage themselves, inhibiting their own marital intimacy.

If there was something lacking in the marriage of our parents, however, there was likely a flaw in their relationship to us as well. As a fifth barrier to marital intimacy, some people seek to compensate for such a parental flaw by seeking a spouse who will undo it. If a parent is perceived as displaying "bad" qualities, the missing good qualities are often wishfully sought in a prospective spouse and can appear as compensation to the son or daughter. Too often, however, after the honeymoon, the "good" qualities disappear and "bad" ones quite like those of their parents seem to displace them. The marriage knot thus appears to bind with an ironic twist, keeping spouses imprisoned in the same kind of inhibited intimacy that they experienced as children.

The sixth obstacle can further complicate this situation and even set it up. That obstacle is protective loyalty to one's parents. This loyalty comes from the deep indebtedness each of us feels for our parents, no matter how much we suffered at home. To protect them from outsiders we must present them as all right. And our spouses are always at first outsiders. There is some degree of this protectiveness in all of us. For some couples, it becomes a way of life.

Part of false loyalty, of course, is self-protective. We tend to forget our most painful memories in order to avoid their pain. But when men and women marry with a truncated, carefully edited, protective awareness of growing up in their families of origin, the stage is set for trouble. One spouse may have an image of growing up that is too good to be true. Underneath it there may be a strong resentment that is suppressed or even repressed, lost to awareness. When the other spouse does not measure up to this hyper-positive image of a perfect lover derived from fictionalized memories of parents, the anger of years past is loosed upon that spouse's head.

Another spouse may realize quite well how he or she suffered from the inadequacies of his or her parents. But the issues are never dealt with in actual contacts with them. While observing conversations between such parents and their offspring, one would surmise that a tacit agreement was in play: "You know what happened and I know what pain resulted, but we'll never talk about it—ever." This is an example of "let bygones be bygones" without reconciliation. It is a barrier to intimacy with one's parents that also inhibits intimacy with one's spouse.

But this avoidance is only wishful thinking, basically like the family history that is too good to be true. The residue of loss, pain, anger, and constriction that has become the legacy of the past remains in escrow. A husband who was smothered by his mother cannot forget his feelings of being humiliated. The memories are etched into his nervous system. And when his wife approaches him in a way reminiscent of his mother, the pressure of the past upsets their intimacy. He feels humiliated again, even when that feeling is not appropriate, when his wife is not smothering him but only seems that way to him because of his earlier experiences.

The seventh barrier is a group of coping techniques, learned from parents by their example, by which members of a family avoid conflict. When two persons come into conflict over some issue, one or both of them seeks to lower the tension by adding a third reality to the situation. This technique is called triangulation. In marital therapy, triangulation often happens as one spouse talks to the therapist, rather than to the other spouse, about problems in the marriage. This indirect way of discussing problems takes the heat off the spouses, but can become a definite obstacle to intimacy, because it deflects their attention and energy away from each other. In marriages such conflict-avoiding triangulation can take different forms. The third reality could be an object such as alcohol, a function such as a profession or employment, a child, or a lover.

Matthew 5:23–24 gives a good example of confronting a triangulation in order to dissolve it. In this case the third reality is religion. Rather than reconciling with our brother, we go to offer a gift at the altar. Jesus in that text deals with conflict-avoidance very much as a marital therapist would. He redirects the person back to deal with the other party to the conflict. Our religious practices are not to be used as ways of avoiding marital intimacy.

We are closing this section with the reference to Matthew's gospel to indicate that we are not dealing with merely worldly concerns here, concerns of mental health and psychological comfort. These are issues of sacramental spirituality as well, of our salvation from sin and death. Our spiritual life is not just, not even primarily, the study and practice of formal prayer. It is our moment-by-moment cooperation with the Spirit in transforming our lives into credible symbols of the presence of God. In matrimony, the "matter" of the sacramental symbol is the couple's sexual intimacy. That is their response to the Spirit in and through the Church. The correct response overcomes the barriers to intimacy mentioned above. And the correct response is the spouses *responding*, rather than *reacting*, to each other. Let us look at this distinction again, for it is crucial, and not always clear. Reactions reinforce these seven barriers to intimacy, but responses remove them. Let us see how.

Reactiveness is quite basic to human life, an inescapable given. Our reactions express what is happening to our bodily systems. Any upset in the balance of our bodily systems gives feedback which arouses a reaction geared to restoring the lost balance. Feedback is automatic and pervasive; it is an adaptive characteristic. Reactions help us cope with threats to our existence and may save our lives. But reactive ability is something we share with the lower animals, in the fight-flight pattern. For instance, Morris the cat will react to discovering another animal eating its cat food. The other animal has threatened Morris' territory and upset the balance of the cat's ecology. If the other animal is a mouse, Morris' fight reaction automatically restores the balance by transforming the intruder into an additional morsel. If Morris perceives a large Doberman pinscher at the food bowl, however, his flight reaction takes over and he relocates to a different, undisturbed environment.

We human beings, especially married folk, have similar, though much more complicated, reactions. Our rationality adds depth, range, reality, and culture as well to our "animal" reactions. But the basic fight-flight pattern remains, as well as the automatic pervasiveness of the reaction. A very crucial narrowing of attention takes over our awareness. We focus only on what will enable us to react more effectively; i.e., what will eliminate the threat and restore our balance. When such a reaction happens in a marriage, the spouse is known only as a threatening object, not as a complete person. Consequently, the marital relation is used to further self-protection rather than intimacy. Spiritually the marriage begins to die.

It may seem melodramatic to use a metaphor of dying in regard to such reactive unions, but the divorce statistics support that view. The legal terminations of marriage simply confirm the spiritual vacuums existing between people who no longer mutually affirm each other. For such couples, love's body has in fact become a body of death and an obstacle to human life. But if they do not comprehend their own reactiveness as a contribution to this breakdown, they are likely to repeat the process later with another sexual partner.

The alternative to this tragic repetition depends upon being able and willing to transcend one's reactions. Such a willingness though, is a very large order, an act of faith requiring openness to grace. Such transcendence requires each spouse to move beyond anxious, uncomfortable reactions to an affirmation of spouse and self in a single act. Such affirmation is the way to live the spirituality of the second great commandment, "Love your neighbor as you love yourself." It is, indeed, the spirituality of Jesus' new commandment,

"Love each other as I have loved you." But a spirituality of love cannot be lived in flight-fight reactiveness. It requires us to be responsive instead.

If we look at how a Catholic marital therapist would help troubled couples to surmount the common barriers to intimacy mentioned above, enabling them to respond rather than react, we can see some basic principles of marital intimacy that all couples might follow. Here the realities of worldly experience can be integrated with a deepening of life in the Spirit so that matrimony comes to be more than a legal structure. The spirituality of matrimony has to deal with and illumine the realities of daily life, including the unpleasant ones. If it does not, the spirituality is empty and not a spirituality at all but probably an intellectual defense of some sort. But if it does, matrimony becomes a sacrament that builds the Church.

Taking the obstacles to intimacy in reverse order, let us look first at conflict avoidance through triangulation. We need to deal with conflict in our spiritual life, for conflict is present throughout the foundational Christian experiences detailed in the gospels. We could even say that our spirituality was forged in conflict and brings "not peace, but the sword" (Matt. 10:34). Our faith is that a conflict can be transformed by grace into new life, but not without cooperative work. Marital therapists try to bring conflicts out in the open, to be negotiated by the spouses. If one or both of the spouses uses work, children, drinking, drugs, a love affair, friends, God, Church, or any other third thing as a diversion from the other, the basic and unavoidable conflicts between the spouses remain untouched. Husband and wife seek such diversion so that they feel less anxious, for no one finds conflict pleasant. Conflicts threaten the intimacy a couple has already established.

Besides, many couples fear that they cannot handle conflict. And they probably cannot; it is too dangerous for them to change. But this fear is one place where the Church must, not only can but must, provide them with help. The Church cannot canonically require matrimony to be a lifetime commitment without providing the resources for couples to learn to resolve the conflicts of that lifetime. Catholic Charities counseling services are already working in this area, but we need to look at these more closely. Catholic Charities marriage counseling should not be "Catholic" in name alone. The current practice places emphasis on the counselors' professional training and certification. Of course, competence is essential. But it does not justify hiring counselors with no regard as to what their own faith commitment or religious development might be.

If we look only for therapeutic competence, we can have the paradoxical situation of a staff of counselors working for the Church who themselves have no training in or personal commitment to the Catholic faith. Counseling based on piety alone, of course, would be incompetent. But marriage counseling based on therapeutic competence alone is not Catholic and might just as well be carried on in a state agency. In order to foster truly sacramental marriages, our counsellors must combine professional competence with well-developed Catholic faith and piety. And these must be truly integrated in the counsellors' minds. For those who keep their beliefs and their professional skills in separate compartments, so that one does not influence the other, cannot foster sacramental marriages either.

Marital therapy helping couples to resolve conflict in a Catholic setting might do some of the same things as in a secular setting. But the motivation and understanding would be different. Catholic couples would be coached in levelling with each other, that is, revealing at appropriate times and places how they feel about themselves, about their messages to each other, and about each other. This therapy is actually a kind of training in responsiveness and in putting aside reactions that assault the spouse (fight) or which run away to where things are safe (flight). Through what is called "boundary keeping" a therapist would supportively teach the spouses to deal with each other rather than talking to the therapist. A therapist might intervene minute by minute in their confrontations with each other, offering them alternative ways of dealing with their pain, ways that were more open and compassionate.

The motivation in doing this coaching would be to facilitate the couple's learning how to "affirm each other as persons." That affirmation is how John Paul II has defined the nature of love. (See Dr. Wilczak's review of his book *Love and Responsibility* in *Marriage Enrichment*, pp. 83–92.) Thus, marital therapy is really training in love. The therapeutic coaching comes to the couple as a grace, a gift, from outside, and strengthens the boundary around their marital relationship. The therapist who is committed to the Catholic faith realizes that the therapy serves as an instrument and symbol of

God's grace. He or she may even pray with clients. The secular therapist does not share this belief. We do not mean to say that God does not heal people through secular, or even atheistic, therapists; God does. But the Church must explicitly cultivate sacramental marriages, proclaiming the gospel in and through the service aspects of marital counselling. Such a specifically Catholic proclamation is implied in the Church's responsiblity to witness marriages.

Catholic therapists, and couples generally, also need to heal the barriers to intimacy found in spouses' relationships with their parents. The first is a false, protective loyalty toward their parents, which may well hide some unresolved anger toward them. This false loyalty needs to be dealt with by each spouse personally with each individual parent. It requires visits to each parent alone, to confront significant experiences and feelings. The purpose of this sometimes gruelling process is an honest reconciliation with parents. And even when a parent had died, there are some techniques that make such reconciliation possible. (Cf. Donald S. Williamson, "New Life at the Graveyard," pp. 94–96.)

Other techniques can heal an attitude of seeing and seeking a spouse as a parent, which comes about by placing one's spouse in charge of one's self-esteem. To heal this attitude, a therapist would encourage the spouse to take responsibility for his or her own self-esteem. We all need to learn how to foster our own self-esteem. When we do well, we can experience our own satisfaction with our own self-set standards. We do not need our spouse's praise to feel good about ourselves. That praise is a wonderful gift and can be received in joy. But we need not feel rotten or worthless without it. Likewise there should be other significant people in our lives, people who appreciate and affirm us as persons besides our spouses. They can lift our spirits when our spouses neglect to. But this means that our spirituality of marriage must include them as well. It will be a communal spirituality because we are communal beings, and community is our natural habitat.

In working through a fear of the opposite sex as threatening, the next obstacle to intimacy, a marital therapist may prescribe specific sexual exercises for definite complaints. Secondary impotence or premature ejaculation in the husband or orgasmic dysfunction in the wife may be the result of a hostility based on fear. Couples can be coached in communicating their resentments and fears, an important part of their intimacy. But more importantly, they can be provided with alternative ways to confront each other sexually, in the very area in which they are most anxious and angry. Sexual desire can heal even these fears, and learning how to cultivate it opens new doors to an intimacy they hadn't dreamed of before.

Therapy that improves a couple's sexual relationship can sometimes reveal yet another obstacle to marital intimacy. The previous obstacle, fear of a spouse as threatening, may stem from a fear of sexual failure, or a fear that the spouse will threaten some dire consequence if the marital partner fails to make love successfully. A couple afflicted with these fears become detached spectators to their own lovemaking, get bogged down in expecting the worst failures, and then live out a self-fulfilling prophecy. There is a vicious circle in which fear of failure causes tension, which causes sexual failure, which then reinforces the fear, to start the circle over again. But there are tasks that can help couples to improve their sexual responsiveness, to open up their spontaneous participation.

If these tasks fail, as they sometimes do, there may be a deeper problem. It may be that what obstructs the intimacy is not fear of failure, but fear of romantic success. It seems odd at first, but it certainly happens that such fear of success arises from anticipating guilt for doing better at intimacy than one's parents have done. As we have said before, this fear is found in good people; it is a consequence of loyalty to their family of origin. Such an overall fear of romantic success would create more specific fears, fears of spontaneity, sexual excitement, and pleasure.

So a number of obstacles to intimacy accumulate and combine here. How can these be dealt with in a spiritually affirming way? One important clue is found in the gospel of John, which emphasizes the sign of water transformed to wine at Cana, the Word made flesh, and the gift of life in abundance. A spirituality based on these strong gospel affirmations of physical life certainly calls us to transform inhibition into success, fear into joy. God calls couples to sexual success in marital love, to live that life of sexual love to the full. But what if they fear such fulfillment?

If their parents did not experience romantic success and sexual satisfaction in marital love, they were, of course, not able to teach their children the skills needed to attain such fulfillment. What we have in mind here are basic skills of attentiveness, empathy, genuineness, self-disclosure, and respect. Marital therapy is one way to learn and develop such skills. But a deeper issue is involved, a symbolic freeing of self from guilt for the fullness of sexual love. Here we return to our reconciliation with our parents, the need to return to them for confrontation and release. In this release, a parent becomes a "former" parent, in a sense, and children grow to the level of peers to those former parents. Parents and their adult offspring enjoy a new intimacy with each other based on mature equality rather than childish dependency and parental control.

Donald S. Williamson described how one of his clients, a clergyman, experienced just such symbolic release:

> striking to him upon reflection . . . was the impact and the movement in the direction of resolution coming from the experience of sitting alone with his father, directly opposite and making continuous eye contact, while discussing issues and problems over the years in the sexual history, sexual identity and sexual experience of the father (p. 94).

Such a confrontation provokes much anxiety for both, but is worth the intense discomfort. As Dr. Williamsom continues:

> The client reported that issues in his own sexuality became more mobile and available to change after face-to-face discussion with the father, in which the facial and other nonverbal cues and tones were available to both parties as certain difficult questions were raised and explored (p. 94).

What happens in these confrontations is that spouses are freed from their fear of intimacy in matrimony through experiencing intimacy with their parents in a decisive way. In this reconciliation and new mutual understanding, the ones who gave us life release us to live our own lives to the full. And the fullness of our sexual intimacy is no longer a threat to them, a criticism of how poorly they did. It is, rather, a fresh gift to them and a hope renewed. For they were our *parents*, and our successes and joys can reflect positively on them, if they are open to this satisfaction.

Our caring to understand them, to appreciate their own struggles, failures, and pains may be a catalyst in this symbolic release. And in the reflected light of our success and joy in love, they may at last be able to say to themselves, "Perhaps I wasn't such a bad parent after all, for love has truly passed between us, a love not afraid to face the truth. And it will live on in the joy of others." In fact, they may also experience a release from their own fears and guilt that will deepen their sexual intimacy too. For their sense of success as parents is a very important element in their self-esteem. And self-esteem is one of the prerequisites of intimacy.

The last two barriers to sexual intimacy—the fear of spontaneity as a threat to one's self-worth, and a feeling that sex is degrading— are related to two features of our American culture. The first is the immaturity of many men and women, which is due to certain cultural values. The second is the absence of any genuine community, which is due to the high mobility of individuals in our society. The first—immaturity—was highlighted over ten years ago, in a psychological study of priests, which concluded that a large proportion of priests are underdeveloped, and that their immaturity reflects that of American men generally (Kennedy and Heckler, p. 7). Although they look mature outwardly, and hold jobs and beget children, many men have not completed the stages of development leading to adulthood. They "have not successfully passed through adolescence" (p. 8).

Such a lack of development is not the result of some inner lack on the part of individuals, however, but rather a feature of our culture. It affects women as well, though perhaps in differing ways. For men in America the passage through adolescence has always been focussed on work. Even today, male identity is still dependent upon work recognition. Who a man is in our culture is largely a matter of what he does for a living. The difference now, however, is that the family base of the breadwinner's identity has been rendered rootless. A man is no longer a working contributor to a community of many families in which he is recognized and appreciated. He is committed instead to an abstraction, to a career, and has become to some extent a professional paladin. The business card of a contemporary man could read: "Have Skills, Will Travel." He can take his family with him, of course, but in doing so uproots them.

The result is often a profound sense of loss of the broader human context needed to affirm and develop a mature identity. Instead of personal development, careerism, or the centering of one's entire identity and life on work, is a common way for men to spend their lives. A family can scarcely compete with work, in size or strength, as a source of identity. And the ability to relocate the family can imply the capacity to displace it as a priority, to put marriage and fatherhood second to one's career. When a man allows such a displacement to occur, however, the situation is very reminiscent of an adolescent rebellion against family constraints.

For an adolescent male, the values of peer groups and organizations leading away from the family, e.g., military service or college, typically become dominant. When something analogous happens with an older man, we wonder whether the displacement of spouse and family by his career might not be simply a continuation of the earlier adolescent process, a process he has not yet completed.

With women today the situation is complicated by the demands of two competing identities. Many women feel obligated to be *both* homemakers *and* wage earners. And if they really want "top grades," they must do the two simultaneously with full-time proficiency. But a person cannot live out such an impossibility for long. Consequently, many women have opted for a variation of the male route to careerism and its liabilities. But for them too, devotion to a career at the expense of their development as persons might just be an adolescent display of "proving themselves" by attaining a status that proves instead to be quite hollow. What men and women need, to be capable of intimacy, is personhood. But how do we develop a positive self-image and a clear sense of identity, in order to become developed, mature persons?

"People who are immature may not need medical or psychological treatment as much as they do need a broader and richer experience of life itself" (Kennedy and Heckler, p. 8). True enough, but too vague to be helpful. Becoming a person with a sense of inner strength means being able to act as a self who is different from, yet meaningfully related to, others. Such unity-in-distinctness, which is the heart and soul of intimacy, is what identity formation yields, and that is what is required for a mature response to vocation, whether it be priesthood, religious vows, or marriage.

The matrix out of which such a sense of self is formed, tested, and confirmed, however, is not the broad sweep of life. A narrower context is required to make possible the richness and closeness of experience and involvement which enables each of us to say: "I am here, a person in my own right, responsibly seeking my own path in this journey with you called life." That narrower context is provided for each of us by our families of origin. The first need, noted above in regard to sexual intimacy, is for persons to be able to become distinct selves, apart yet connected emotionally, vis-a-vis the families in which they have grown up.

What this growth process largely boils down to is learning to relate as a responsible adult to our own parents. If this is not done, we will use marriage (or perhaps ordination) as a rite of initiation into adult identity. And marriage or ordination will break down under the strain. It is a recognized but largely unappreciated fact that contemporary American culture does not possess a ritual means to enter into adulthood and be communally affirmed as an adult. (For some thoughtful comment on this lack see Salvador Minuchin, "Adolescence: Society's Response and Responsibility," pp. 455–76, and Mark Gerzon, *The Whole World Is Watching: A Young Man Looks at Youth's Dissent,* pp. 208–217.) Consequently, marriage has been used inappropriately as a rite of passage.

Erik H. Erikson's developmental psychology clearly explains the inappropriateness of this practice, for marriage ritually "fits" the *sixth* stage of life. An adult identity, however, is the appropriate achievement of the *fifth* stage, adolescence. Mature personal identity provides the foundation for marital intimacy between two adult selves. Persons who have not achieved this firm, mature identity typically rely on a significant other for affirmation as a self. In marriage this reliance results in the balance of overdependencies in which "She makes me feel like a man/He makes me feel like a woman." Responsibility for one's self-esteem is handed over to the marital partner. Likewise, when marital intimacy becomes troubled, responsibility for bad feelings about one's self is placed on the other person: "It's *your* fault that I'm so unhappy, miserable, dissatisfied, etc."

But the responsibility for feelings about one's self must be taken back and owned by the self. Each one of us is responsible for building and maintaining our own self-esteem. But in order to assume that responsibility, we need to resolve certain basic issues in our own families of origin and bring them to sufficient closure. They include a sense of effective competence; a transcendence of disappointed desire; sexual integration; and loyalty sustained by justice, love, and reconciliation.

We attain a sense of effective competence by mastering certain skills that are crucial for adult life. Erikson has provided us with a helpful list of "vital virtues" or strengths, each one marking a stage of human development: hope, will, purpose, competence, fidelity, love, care, and wisdom. (See his *Insight and Responsibility,* pp. 111–134.) Family therapist Virginia Satir would add that at least one parent must celebrate the child's progress on this ladder of strengths for the child to develop the self-esteem based on his mastery of these skills. If both parents celebrate his growth, so much the better. The celebration consists in 1) noting each developmental step, 2) affirming the child for the progress, and 3) providing the child with increasing opportunity to practice the new abilities developed (Virginia Satir, *Conjoint Family Therapy: A Guide to Theory and Technique,* pp. 46–47). In this way, parents serve as coaches in the effective competence on which their child's future sexual intimacy can be based.

The transcendence of desire has to do with childhood disappointments in relationships with parents. What if a parent did not validate the development of a child? The child's sense of self, and self-esteem, will be deficient. He will wonder if perhaps he was unworthy of the validation that he needed. He will seek for someone else who can satisfy his deep need for such affirmation. He will look for another person to establish his self-worth. He will develop a skewed and one-sided model of the original parent as "bad" while seeking someone to be the "good" parent.

Although this model can be far from obvious to the people involved, it can serve tacitly as a strong motive in the search for a spouse. What usually happens in such a search is that the chosen spouse can and does function as "good" parent for a while, but in time is experienced as "bad." It is remarkable how marriages repeat the dissatisfactions of the parents of the spouses. The way to heal this tendency is to confront the disappointed desire for intimacy with our parents in its original context. That is, if we can come to be reconciled with our parents, in genuine intimacy with them, we will not need to look on our spouses as substitute sources of our own self-esteem.

The third basic issue that we need to resolve with our parents in order to be capable of marital intimacy is our sexual integration—one of the main areas in which children find disappointed desires that need to be transcended. This disappointment is very common, because both parents must be involved in the validation process, and one cannot make up for the withdrawal of the other (Satir, pp. 48–54). Both parents must communicate to their children of both sexes that the children are esteemable persons of the gender that they are, in spite of not being of the other gender.

This message can come verbally but must be conveyed nonverbally to be credible. The children must be treated as esteemable sexual persons. But even more crucially, the parents must treat each other that way in their own marital relationship. They must practice what they preach. Otherwise sexuality will remain nonintegrated, a shameful residue, a source of inescapable burden and discrimination. Psychoanalytic terms such as "penis envy," "castration complex," and "conversion hysteria" are attempts to comprehend such sexual nonintegration. It is a lack of esteem either for one's own gender identity or for that of the opposite sex.

But what if this challenge is not successfully met within the family? Let's consider the fourth of the issues that adults must resolve with their parents in order to be capable of sexual intimacy. We have described this last issue as a sense of loyalty to one's family of origin, but a loyalty sustained by justice, love, and reconciliation. The last element, reconciliation, is the key emphasis and spiritual foundation of this total process of personal maturity. Reconciliation is also a major task in married life, and thus a theme in any marital spirituality. Reconciliation with one's parents as a prerequisite to marital intimacy is one instance of what the gospel recommends:

> If, when you are bringing your [self as] gift to the altar [in the sacrament of matrimony], you suddenly remember that your [father, mother, sister or] brother has a grievance against you [and/or you against them], [take] leave [of giving] your [self as] gift, [to another] . . . before the altar. First go and make your peace [i.e., become reconciled] with your [father, mother, sister or] brother, and only then come back and offer your gift. (Adapted from the translation in *The New English Bible*, Matt. 5:23–24.)

This kind of reconciliation, in any deep sense, would be very difficult for anyone, parent or child. But those who achieved it would be sure that they were not using marriage as a ticket out of the family of origin or as a rite of initiation into adulthood. For many people such a deep reconciliation would likely be accomplished after the wedding, because it takes a long time. Only then would a genuine sexual intimacy be possible for them.

Some of family therapist Murray Bowen's research indicates the possibility and value of this kind of reconciling return to one's parents even after one's marriage is already underway. In the years 1967 to 1969 Dr. Bowen noted that a group of his psychiatric residents who had been doing family-of-origin work with their own families were superior as a group to those who were not—in two fundamental ways. They were better clinicians, and they made as much progress improving their own marriages as did other residents who were in formal therapy with their spouses. He had not expected such a result. And in his own words, "This surprise development was a turning point in my professional life" (Murray Bowen, *Family Therapy in Clinical Practice*, p. 532).

Bowen's discovery has spiritual as well as psychological importance. All of us feel a deep, abiding loyalty to our families of origin, a oneness with kin. This unity itself is a spiritual function, since spirit can be called the principle of unity in human action. In fact, Jesus sent his Spirit so that all of us might be one. But if basic dissatisfactions in the marriage of our parents interfered with their abilities to validate us as developing persons, our loyalty to them tends to block us from two spiritual goals. The first is freedom, the second, hope. The consequence is a spirituality turned against itself, so that married life can lead to disunity instead of unity. Freedom turns into captivity (cf. Gail E. Chandler, *The Family as Spiritual Community*, pp. 37–43), and hope turns into despair (cf. W. Robert Beavers and Florence W. Kaslow, *The Anatomy of Hope*, pp. 119–26).

The marital pain of our parents can in a sense capture us, deprive us of freedom. If they had problems with intimacy, we tend to experience our own growth and joy in intimacy as disloyal to them. The realization of our potential to accomplish what they did not appears as a kind of injustice or oneupmanship. We thus, out of loyalty to them, hold ourselves back from opportunities to grow beyond them in sexual intimacy. We are not free to be successfully intimate without feeling guilty. We may even shrink from the possibilities of doing better than they did.

The other side of this holding back, of course, is the part of our parents that does not want us to do better either. They may feel jealous of us. The ancient teaching that we are all sinners is based partly on the commonness of envy. This theme is woven through biblical narratives, from the Cain and Abel story to the passion accounts in the New Testament. We should not be surprised, then, to find the pattern in our parents, and in ourselves as well. The accepting and supporting of someone else to do better than we have done demands a work of spiritual catharsis, an emptying of self that is an effect and gesture of grace. It calls for parents and their adult children to confront each other in altruistic love, identifying each other's maximum marital intimacy as their own happiness and joy. Such a kenosis is only possible through grace. When it happens, it is a part of the grace of the sacrament of matrimony.

Secondly, against a background of defective intimacy in the marriage of our parents, and their failure to validate our sexual self-esteem, we do not have much basis for hope in a better future, because our intimacy skills are largely derived from the model that our parents provided. Thus a perverted kind of justice ties us to their failures and limitations, and tends to perpetuate these across the generations. It may even seem unthinkable to admit that we need to learn what they were unable to teach us. With this admission, however, and openness to learning from persons beyond the family, persons in the broader communal environment, we can nurture alternatives which are more free and hopeful. Such nurture can lead to personal transformation, so that we can live in freedom and hope despite the failures of our parents.

Let us use the example of a Catholic couple coached by Dr. Wilczak in marital therapy for over a year. During their work with him the wife became increasingly aware that she had received two basic yet unrealistic messages from her parents, especially her mother: 1) men are a pain in the behind, and 2) sex is not fun. When she and her husband began therapy they were experiencing constant unproductive quarrels and very little enjoyment in their sexual relations. As the wife became more aware of how her mother's beliefs served as her own self-fulfilling prophecy, she became angry at her mother. This anger served her very well as a basis for self-differentiation and personal responsibility.

She began to allow herself to learn that her mother was wrong and in fact had also suffered from her false beliefs regarding men and sex. This enabled the daughter to be open to and accepting of experiences that contradicted her mother's messages. This in turn helped her to be reconciled with her mother as a woman burdened by many troubles and doubts that she struggled to cope with in a blaming, hostile, and self-denying way. The consequence was new freedom and hope in the daughter's own marital relationship.

The spiritual importance of such a transformation, of course, is that obstacles to marital intimacy and satisfaction are blocks to the functioning of the sacramental symbol. Sacraments cause what they symbolize, but only to the extent that their symbolism is accurate. Sexual love causes joyous and ecstatic communion between persons, but only to the extent that it is joyous and ecstatic. If it is not, it is not a cause of our intimacy with Father, Son and Spirit, of their living in us and us in them. If one spouse believes that persons of the opposite sex are a pain, that sexual relations are a burden, the symbolism of matrimony becomes truncated and perverted. The spouses then interact in a way that cuts them off from the joys to which they are called by God, perhaps even with feelings that they do not deserve such joys. And their sexual relationship tends to become an instrument of hostility and even hatred, rather than intimacy.

Such a use of hostile sex is indeed a hard core sexual perversion. (See Robert J. Stoller, *Perversion*, p. 4.) Life within such distressed marriages takes on the qualities of one of the oldest symbols of evil, the net or snare in which we are fatally trapped. (See Paul Ricoeur, *The Symbolism of Evil*, pp. 81–99.) A central goal of marital spirituality, then, is to transform the snare into the net of salvation, the symbol of the ministry of the disciples of Jesus. These very bonds of suffering in marriage are to be converted sacramentally into life-giving ties with God, who is love.

CHAPTER **IV**

THE MISSION OF
SEXUAL INTIMACY

But if this conversion of the marriage trap into the tie that binds is to really come about, we must heal another defect in our culture, the absence of any genuine community beyond couples and families. Marital intimacy needs to be nurtured and enriched by a broader communal covenant with the Lord. In this bonding, in which the intimacy of couples both sustains and is sustained by the larger community, we have the connection between matrimony and the Church as the basic sacrament of Christ. Such a bonding is countercultural, however. It requires us to see marriages, and human relationships in general, as covenants rather than contracts. Contracts are based upon power—their participants possess power, and agree to restrain it in return for certain benefits. Contracts are enforced by power too; their violators are punished by a loss of power.

Covenants, by contrast, are based on love. Their partners seek each other's welfare in mutual altruism. Violators of covenants are met by a loving willingness to forgive, seventy times seven times. But in our society, the very idea of a covenant community seems strange and alien. Almost every adult relationship is contractual. Work, recreation, even marriages, involve people in contracts—exchanges of goods and services, rights and obligations, payments to be rendered. Such human relationships are superficial and fragmented; they clearly and severely limit the commitments of people to each other's well-being. They amount to a commercializing of human relations that makes intimacy impossible.

A covenant, though, is radically different. People in a covenant are linked by *hesed,* by God's own tender, forgiving, steadfast love. The bond of covenant love is symbolized in the Bible by shared blood, the blood of the paschal victim poured out. This symbol of shared blood is realized in our common life in the Spirit—an authentic bodily and communal life in which we must love each other, here and now, because God first loved us through his Son (1 John 4: 8–10).

This sensuous, concrete, immediacy so central to Johannine spirituality directly relates to married life as a sacrament, in two ways. First, married life is lived out in an everyday unity of verbal and nonverbal communication, i.e., human interaction, which is the ongoing matter and form of the sacrament. Unity must be acted out across the whole sweep of life; it cannot live merely within people's minds and hearts. Sacramental symbols have to be perceived—heard or seen, tasted, touched. Secondly, married life is essentially connected with the life of the entire Christian community by way of the covenant, that is, by connection with the Church as a covenant community, which is the fundamental sacrament. Through this connection couples receive support from and give enrichment to that wider covenantal community. And in this covenantal connection with what amounts to a spiritual ecology, people experience the presence of God, of triune intimacy.

This view seems rather abstract, idealistic, neat, "too good," in a way. In real life, sacramental love is enacted within a less stable context, one patterned by both *grace* and *sin.* Our faith asserts, though, that grace has triumphed over sin. But sin remains an amazingly powerful factor, a truly lethal threat to sexual intimacy. All forms of human life can be destroyed by sin, including marriage. Such a statement may sound anachronistic. No self-respecting, agnostic humanist would dare to take such a medieval proposition seriously. But we must part company with the humanist psychotherapists here, and purely secular views of marriage, if we are to live according to the gospel. The good news of faith does bring the gift of life, but against the background of a lethal "something" which is called sin. The gospel calls our attention to both patterns, grace and the desperate need for grace to counteract sin.

The patterns of grace are prior, however, and will win out. We would like to consider these empirically from the perspective of contemporary personal values. Karol Wojtyla has specified these as effective "self-determination," personal "transcendence," and somatic-psychical "integration." (See *The Acting Person,* pp. 66, 115–124, 149–152, 189–92, 196–99, 206–210, 255–58, 264–67, 320–23.) These abstract philosophical terms, used by the Archbishop of Crakow to describe personal growth, refer to the very same realities that we have been considering as the basis of marital intimacy; persons must make the transition to adulthood not through marriage, but before marriage, at least in some basic way. Only then do we have a gift, a self, to offer at the altar of matrimony.

But that passage to adulthood requires us to become effectively self-determined, to establish our identities as loving persons with solid self-esteem, by our own choice and not in adolescent or childish dependence on a sexual partner. That passage calls for personal transcendence—the decentering of our love from ourselves to other people whom we identify as our *other* selves. And it requires us to achieve a basic body-soul integration, a wholeness of mind, body, and emotions that does not suppress any of these.

In making this passage to adulthood, we will overcome the barriers to sexual intimacy that we mentioned earlier: contempt for sexuality, fear of spontaneity, hostility toward the opposite sex, conflict-avoidance, and the unresolved issues between us and our parents. No one, of course, achieves such maturity in any complete way. But the basic passage ought to be made before one takes wedding vows. The vows then would be promises of mutual support in the ongoing quest for greater maturity as the basis for deepening sexual intimacy.

In summary, a person experiences self-fulfillment through effective self-determination, personal transcendence or authentic growth, and an integration of bodily capacities and achievements. But performance of these values (and they are values only as performed) comes only through participation with other persons who support and foster each other's growth. Individuals cannot do it alone; nor can couples, or even families. We need a much broader community; we need intimacy on the broadest scale that we can manage, for the more we extend love to our other selves, the more fulfilled we become. We must, then, look at marriage in its larger context of society and Church. Growth in intimacy is what ought to happen in marriage. But it cannot happen in a marriage that is a "closed system." Yet such marriages are precisely what our culture offers today. The British psychiatrist Henry V. Dicks sums up our situation as follows:

> The urban family is almost self-liquidating by dispersal, just when in their isolation they need each other most among the frightening impersonality of modern industry and commerce. . . .
>
> Technological society puts much pressure on families to prepare their children for *in*dependence, or at least spurious standing on their own feet, to earn their living far from their family of origin.
>
> For human and marital success it is, I maintain, equally necessary to conserve and make available in adult life the toleration of the opposite qualities—tender concern for others based on one's own, still felt, dependent needs. Otherwise the "I'm all right, Jack" posture will oust the "love thy neighbor as thyself" aim in our community. The open, giving, because secure, personality would be replaced by the anxiously taking, shut-in, suspicious personality, if the prevailing attitude of the small, closed nuclear family transmitted its defensive island mentality to its children. (*Marital Tensions*, pp. 29–30)

This replacement has already occurred on a large scale, particularly in America. It is one of the broad, communal patterns that sacramental couples must counteract, in order to extend the victory of grace over sin. This task is of absolutely vital significance; it is not an option that we can overlook. For the prevailing situation is deeply eroding the basic human capacities and values that are the conditions of the possibility of both marital commitment and personal fulfillment. Our culture as it is now will lead soon to the gradual extinction of life in community. The term may still be used, but the real interconnectedness, continuing concern, and daily personal interaction will have disappeared. In their place we will have a complex of commercial and contractual transactions without the care that identifies the mutual giving and receiving of persons sharing life. The ethical and spiritual impact of this state of affairs is tremendous. Here is a description of what our culture, our life, will become:

> What the loss of a sense of community involves—and involves not abstractly but quite concretely—is the loss of the ability to imagine that one's actions have any consequence outside one's own life. Once this has taken place, certain priorities follow: among them, the accompanying loss of the ability to imagine anything more important than one's own happiness. The firm reign of the idea of the greatest happiness for oneself as the sole standard for judging one's own conduct is only one result of the withered sense of community in contemporary life (Joseph Epstein, *Divorced in America*, p. 95).

> In this situation marriage has, inevitably, lost its special character as something sacred, as it once was even to the unreligious, and as a relationship contracted for life. Marriage today is nothing more than another possibility—one among many. The idea of permanence in marriage is fast going by the boards—in an age where the possible predominates, everyone becomes a temporary person (p. 97).

In this situation, personal values, even for the isolated individuals seeking them with all their strength, are choked out. The redundant sequences of behavior antithetical to the performance of those values within our social systems have taken over. The loss of community leads to a selfishness that erodes community even more, and the vicious circle goes on. The sure result will be the lethal web of evil, the snare of sin, two ancient metaphors from the history of religions, in which we are caught.

And the only opportunity existing today to counteract this deadly process rests with the last vestiges of community yet existing, the churches. They are the only social organizations that value community *per se* as "the people of God," the "Body of Christ," or the "communion of saints." Consequently, they are the only organizations that can take a value-based stance that could offer an authentic alternative to the current malaise. Every other approach would merely "use" community to mask a rescue of the "greatest happiness for oneself" as a norm and eventually corrupt us into a house divided against itself, one which cannot stand.

The churches must confront and renew their own values so as to create the communal spiritual ecology out of which the spirituality of real married couples can take nurture—and we mean real nurture, not legal stricture. We mean ongoing involvement with the needs, troubles, trials, and failures of living people *as they are happening,* not merely as a kind of mop-up ministry after the fact. For all the good intentions, admirable skill, and real dedication involved, a significant aspect of ministry to the divorced is precisely such an "after-the-fact" ministry.

What we are urging must come much sooner, and is implied in the responsible witnessing of marriages by official representatives of the Church. This sacramental function of witnessing needs to be continued beyond the wedding liturgy and needs to be extended throughout the marriage in continuing service to couples: counseling, training and formation aimed at fostering sexual intimacy. We need a continuing respectful presence of the faith community to married people, and coaching that will help them to live out a spirituality that supportively challenges them to transcend their individual reactiveness to each other.

Each couple must be challenged instead to respond to each other in a way that fosters the personalistic values mentioned earlier. But they must respond not merely for the values themselves, but ultimately as a symbolic realization of the One who is preeminently person, God. For this is the "great" commandment—to love the source of all our human loves and the font of every personal value. And in this marvelous interplay that marks the communal life of faith, hope, and love, we witness to the Spirit who calls us all to eternal life.

Some recent researchers see a glimmer of hope for our culture. Daniel Yankelovitch, in a recent extensive study of the attitudes of younger Americans, found that their own experience was leading them to question the dominant patterns of our culture:

> Among the people I interviewed, many truly committed self-fulfillment seekers focus so sharply on their own needs that instead of achieving the more intimate relationships they desire, they grow farther apart from others. In dwelling on their own needs, they discover that the inner journey brings loneliness and depression. They are caught in a debilitating contra-

diction: their goal is to expand their lives by reaching beyond the self, but the strategy they employ constricts them, drawing them inward toward an ever-narrowing, closed-off "I." People want to enlarge their choices but, seeking to "keep all options open," they diminish them (*New Rules in American Life*, p. 40).

Yankelovitch is, of course, a secular researcher. But he very nearly quotes the Bible *verbatim* in his conclusion: "The injunction that to find oneself one must lose oneself contains a truth any seeker of self-fulfillment needs to grasp" (p. 50). (Cf. Mark 8:35; Matt. 10:39 and 16:25; Luke 9:24.)

Among these young people who have experienced the isolation, frustration and lack of fulfillment brought by a self-centered search for one's own happiness, oblivious to the happiness of others, Yankelovitch also found a new way of life forming:

The conventional strategy of the search for self-fulfillment is based on the calculus of inner needs. In the new ethic of social commitment . . . this strategy is replaced by a deeper reaching outward. The new ethic recognizes that self-fulfillment requires commitments that endure over long periods of time and that the expressive and sacred domains can be realized only through a web of shared meanings that transcend the conception of the self as an isolated physical object (p. 89).

The motivation for this new mode of life seems still to be basically selfish, a search for committed relationships with others for the sake of one's own personal fulfillment. We have seen that this subtler form of self-seeking is as destructive of intimacy as is a more blatant use of other people for one's own benefit. But some young people seem, at least, to be trying to take a step in the right direction. This change may well be the work of the Spirit of God in our world, challenging us to cooperate. It is, then, imperative that Catholic married couples work harder than ever to overcome the barriers to sexual intimacy, and that we do so in a context of support for that intimacy by the whole Church.

An example of such support would be the celebration of marriages. We don't mean wedding ceremonies, but the actual lives of married couples in the community. Such communal celebration of marriages would call for two important renunciations, which would be transformed into an appreciation and ongoing emotional support of actual married couples. The first "renunciation" is something each of us had to attain in our own families of origin. Psychiatrist W. Robert Beavers locates it in our transcending of sexual desire for the parent of the opposite sex, the classical Oedipal conflict:

> Why is renunciation so necessary in resolving the Oedipal conflict? One can have a parent, one can have a lover, but one cannot have a father or mother and a lover in the same person. If it is not clear whether one has a parent or a lover, he has neither. Here is another central human paradox: By renouncing, one can receive (*Psychotherapy and Growth*, p. 140).

And this, too, is another secular brush with the gospel, a concrete step toward giving up our life in order to find it.

This first renunciation is a growing appreciation of the value of the exclusive sexual love between our parents. Their sexual love, satisfaction, and joy are no longer taken by us, their children, as a threat or deprivation, but as a foundation for their very real but different parental love for us. We are freed by their firm and satisfying love to seek our own sexual fulfillment outside the family in a mature, hopeful, loving commitment. The second renunciation is our commitment to, in and for a community, so that we work to enhance the intimacy and romantic success of other couples as our own communal enrichment. This joyous love of others likewise does not threaten or deprive us but rather enriches us with its evocative power. When we and our communities deeply celebrate the marriages of our fellow Catholics, we will challenge each other, in love and support, to the real give and take of marriage.

Our faith communities, thus, must become involved in the issues, concerns, and values of the life of sexual love. We cannot in conscience merely surrender this area to the secular sex therapists. It is too central to the sacrament of matrimony for that. For if we do not get involved, we leave couples subject to the influences of a society that masks a destructive, fearful selfishness with the superficial glamour of a media-touted "sexual revolution."

The eminent psychiatrist and sex therapist Helen Singer Kaplan sums up this situation as follows:

> The fear of intimacy is highly prevalent in our society and may produce problems that extend beyond sexual dysfunctions. We

tend to spectate rather than participate together, watch TV, play cards and video games rather than engage in intimate conversation. It sometimes seems that people are more afraid of intimacy than they are of sex. They find it easier to masturbate than to make love, to buy impersonal sex than to share love with a lover, to blot out the partner with drugs than to experience him/her fully (*Disorders of Sexual Desire*, pp. 183–84).

We believe our faith communities must counteract this situation of fear, this promotion of pseudointimacy through the media as an opiate for its members. We need to develop an entirely different approach to fostering the practical spirituality of marital love, which is the deepening of sexual intimacy. Such an approach may at first seem frightening, even repulsive or anti-Christian to us, but should be carefully, thoughtfully, and faithfully worked out anyhow. It may require married couples' retreats which include very concrete and specific guidance in sexual relating, under the supervision of competent Christian professionals. Such guidance is a badly needed part of what has elsewhere been called "supporting the spiritual carnality of Christian marriage" (Paul F. Wilczak, "The Fullness of Physical Love," pp. 13–25, in *Marriage Enrichment*). We may need to use some of the techniques developed by professional marital therapists, i.e., the use of explicit films or tapes of sexual relating, and carefully supported and guided sexual exercises for married couples during such retreats.

This guidance can be done in a prayerful, nonthreatening, and authentically Christian manner. And in the doing of this very special and needed retreat ministry, the marriages thus challenged and sustained would in turn be prepared to better "edify" or build up their communities, spiritually as well as emotionally. They would be helped to witness more clearly to the viability of sexual love, not only in itself, but as a symbol that both participates in and points to the divine Love. For human love-play is the causal symbol which draws us into the love-play of the Trinity, and it into us. It is a sacrament that builds the Church by transfiguring spouses into credible symbols of the God who is love.

The interplay between couples and their larger society, though, which fosters intimacy, moves in both directions. Couples who enjoy a genuine sexual intimacy play a powerful role in constructing the very community that supports them, the Church. Let us look more closely now, at the dynamics of this process, at how, precisely, the causal symbol of matrimony builds the Church. For that edification is the mission of the married. It is possible because of the inborn need of all persons for intimacy in every aspect of life, not just *vis-à-vis* a spouse.

God created us for love, for he knows that love alone brings us purpose and identity. He who is love (1 John 4:8) calls us to enter into an ever-growing awareness of our being loved infinitely by the family of three self-giving Persons—Father, Son and Holy Spirit. In experiencing God's triune love for us, we are guided into our true identity and meaning. But what, exactly, is this triune love? Since happiness for any human being is a participation in that, we need to understand, as best we can, what the inner life of God is like. God made us in his image; thus divine and human intimacy mirror each other, and each can help us to understand the other. Let us look, then, to our trinitarian model.

One good but not very well-known description of the Trinity, based on a comparison to human love, is in Richard of St. Victor's book, *On the Trinity*. Here we see human and divine love mirroring each other in such a way that the human experience of love in marriage reveals something about the inner life of the Trinity, while the divine revelation of the Trinity is a model for married life and human intimacy generally. Richard thus shows that God could not be a single person, a mind and will isolated from all other minds and wills, but is an Intimacy in which three divine persons know and love each other, respond and relate to each other, exchange selves with each other in an infinitely and eternally perfect way. Each Person—Father, Son, Spirit—enjoys an infinitely perfect understanding of the others. Each loves the others with perfect benevolence and generosity, totally willing the goodness of the others without any shadow of jealousy or selfishness. And each is perfectly understood, loved, accepted and enjoyed by the others.

Richard, in fact, uses human love to show that God cannot be a single person, just as a human being cannot love in isolation. The main feature of love is self-transcendence, going beyond concern for oneself, decentering one's attention and concern. We recognize in our human experience that a person who is totally self-centered is deficient in love. God the Father, then, cannot be the only divine

Person. There must be at least one other to whom his love can go; otherwise he would be unable to transcend his own egoism, to love beyond himself. He would be unable to love. Since the world, as his creature and thus inferior to him, is not adequate to receive the love that the Father has to give, there must be a second divine Person—someone who is infinitely perfect, and thus able to receive the infinite love of the Father, someone who is on a par with him in understanding and love. That someone is the Father's Son.

Two Persons are not enough, however. Referring again to human experience, Richard finds that love that is restricted to two persons is still a deficient love; for in such cases, either the two love each other exclusively, in a selfishness *à deux* that violates the nature of love, a mutual egoism; then they love no one else, care for no one else except each other. And that is deficient love. Or else, each insists that the beloved give love to no one except himself, and receive love from no other. Their love, in other words, is jealous. And jealousy is a fault, a defect in human love.

Father and Son, being infinitely perfect in their love, can display no such jealousy. Each wants the other to love and be loved beyond himself. They seek, then, to share their mutual love with utter generosity, to pour it out on some third reality. Once again that third cannot be some created reality, even all of creation. It must be divine, on a par with Father and Son, able to receive with infinite understanding and love the infinite love that Father and Son have to give. According to Richard's analysis, then, there must be a third person in God, the Spirit of the Father and the Son.

The divine intimacy thus has three members. God is a Trinity, a triune intimacy in which Father, Son and Spirit share their very selves in perfect mutual understanding and love, with no shadow of selfishness or jealousy. But with these three, the Godhead is complete. There is no fourth or fifth person in God because love reaches its highest possible perfection in these three. The Father transcends himself completely in loving an infinite Son, and Father and Son share their mutual love completely in their infinite Spirit.

Love can never be static or reach an end. It is always a burning desire to stretch out in greater and greater transcendence to find oneself in self-surrender to another. Thus God, as his divine revelation makes known to us in Holy Scripture, even goes beyond the self-contained, circular movement within the Trinity. The love of the three divine persons for each other goes out to creation, and especially to us humans, created by God with the ability to share in the divine self-communicating love. The author of the Book of Genesis explains in simple language how the immanent, personalized relationships within God move outward toward the human race to share those same triune, family relationships with us human beings: "God said, 'Let us make man in our own image, in the likeness of ourselves' " (Gen. 1:26).

By God's own gracious gift, we enter into the divine Intimacy itself, beginning at our baptism a process of growth that never ends. This process is what the early Greek Fathers called *divinization (theosis)* or the process of a human person becoming truly a participator in God's very own nature (2 Pet. 1:4). By God's "uncreated energies of love," his triune, personalized, loving actions in the self-giving of Father, Son and Holy Spirit to us, we receive created grace. We become God's own children, "born not out of human stock or urge of the flesh or will of man but of God himself" (John 1:12–13). "The Spirit himself and our own spirit bear united witness that we are children of God" (Rom. 8:16; Gal. 4:6–7). We can now love each other with the unique love of the Father, Son and Holy Spirit. As we love each human being whom we are privileged in time and space to meet, we allow God's love on this earth to become more complete and more clearly manifested. ". . . but as long as we love one another, God will live in us and his love will be complete in us" (1 John 4:12).

Not only do we perfect or complete God's loving action among us, but in a sense we also complete God's love within the Trinity. God the Father, in his Spirit, loves the Son, Jesus Christ. From all eternity God loved his Son and comprehended him in the triune love that would be outpoured into the human race through the Incarnation, as the Son became forever a part of that human race. The Father, thus, can never love the Son alone, but as he is the Logos in whom the whole world, "all things in heaven and on earth" (Col. 1:16), have been created (John 1:3). The Father loves his total Son, Christ. Each of us is a part of Christ now by our having been created according to his image and likeness. At our baptism into his Body, the Church, the Spirit comes to dwell within us, the source of oneness in his Body. "There is one Body, one Spirit, just as you were all called into one and the same hope when you were called. There is one Lord, one faith, one baptism, and one God who is Father of all, over all, through all and within all" (Eph. 4:4–6).

The Father waits for the spirit in us to respond with Christ, our Head, so that together in the Spirit of love we can call him *our* Father. Father and Son, along with the hidden Spirit, are in a way incomplete until we consciously accept our identity in their love and return this love to them. The love of the Father for the Son, the love that draws us with Christ into the life of the Trinity, includes us as well, for we are the mission of Jesus, and we are commissioned (co-missioned) to extend it throughout the world: "As you have sent me into the world, I have sent them into the world" (John 17:18). This specific inclusion of finite persons created by God into the salvific mission of his Son is the foundation for our spiritual lives, the imitation of Christ. Just as Our Lord emptied himself of manifest "equality with God" to enter and experience our natural world as one of us (Phil. 2:6–9), we too must empty ourselves. Just as by passing "through the test of suffering" God came to us all in our bodily suffering (Heb. 2:14–18), we can follow his path in empathy, passing through the test in order to reach the glory of full intimacy.

What we really communicate then, when we love—when we exchange selves in our human intimacy—is the life of God himself, the exchange of selves in mutual altruism that *is* trinitarian life. That life is what grace is. That life is what we give to each other when we love, our intimacy with God. That life is what we receive from each other when we are loved. And that life is what is already in us, before we begin to love, making it possible for us to freely accept the grace that God offers. Grace makes us intimates of each other in the Church, and as the Church, intimates with divine Intimacy. This exchange of graced selves, this communication of trinitarian intimacy through human intimacy, is the life mission of every baptized person. Such love is *kenotic,* an abandonment and emptying of self out of altruistic concern for another, resembling the *kenosis* that the Son underwent when he accepted the Incarnation.

But this common baptismal mission takes a special form in matrimony. Good communication—responsiveness rather than reactiveness—is essential as the technique of human intimacy. Responsive communication is also essential as the technique of sexual intimacy that is the heart of the sacramental symbol of matrimony. Thus we can learn something about the Trinity by looking at responsiveness in marriage, and something about responsiveness in a marriage by looking at the Trinity. Responsive communication calls for attentiveness to the one we love. That attentiveness, with slow, relaxed looking at, listening to, and touching each other, is, as we have seen, part of the structure of confrontations that are the alternative to reactive attacks. And attentiveness is absolutely crucial to successful love-making, the kind that brings both spouses to ecstatic self-abandon. It is indeed a kind of *kenosis*—a decentering of attention from self to beloved, an abandonment of self to another's need and possible control. Such a *kenosis* is a modest reflection of the *kenosis* of Jesus, who, though he was divine, did not consider divinity something to cling to (Phil. 2:6). He let it go, being obedient even unto death, so that we might have life, and have it more abundantly (John 10:10).

Thus any act of human generosity, benevolence, or attentive concern is modelled on, and reflects, the *kenosis* of the Son. But marital generosity, benevolence, attentive concern—especially in sexual intercourse—are more than reflections or mere symbols of the *kenosis*. These are sacramental symbols, symbols that effectively cause what they symbolize. Sexual intercourse, then, is an enactment of the intimacy of the baptized couple with each other and with the triune God. But it is also a causal symbol of their intimacy with all mankind. Matrimony builds the Church. Let us try to understand ecclesial intimacy more deeply, and more concretely.

The first way that the sacrament of matrimony works to build the Church is by transforming spouses so deeply, and so obviously, that the result can only be called a transfiguration, similar to the transfiguration experienced by Jesus on Mount Tabor. The process is the process of redemption, of reversing and healing the effects of original sin so that our final state—our redeemed, transfigured state—is even better than what we might have been if there had been no original sin.

Modern psychology, with its discoveries about mental health and emotional maturity, can help us to understand this transfiguring process. Selfishness is the essence of sinfulness, and our persistent, deep tendency to be selfish is the state of original sin in which we are all born. We begin to emerge from it at our baptism, which is our initiation into the community of those who have promised to help each other with that emergence, thereby forming themselves into a communion of intimates. When we speak of selfishness, however, we are not just referring to a kind of stinginess and self-seeking, such as that of the child who wants for himself the first and biggest portion of the family dinner. That kind of selfish immaturity is a part of what we need to be transfigured out of, of course; but it is not our deepest sinfulness. That deep sinfulness, which is our constant tendency, can more or less poison even the good things that we do, and is so deep and terrible that its healing required the death of the Son of God on the cross.

This deep selfishness is what psychologists refer to as narcissism, egoism, or self-centeredness. Narcissism is the attitude of Narcissus, the character in the Greek myth who accidentally caught sight of his own reflection in a pool of water and became totally captivated by it. He was so fascinated by his own reflection that he didn't notice anything or anyone else. He lost track of time, forgot to eat and sleep, and finally became literally rooted to the spot—transformed into the flower that we now call the Narcissus.

Our narcissism is a deep and constant egoism, our tendency to be fascinated with ourselves, to focus our attention on ourselves; it is our way of seeing the world totally in relation to ourselves, our inability to realize the importance, the genuine importance, of other persons. To the degree that we remain self-centered, we may easily develop other traits of character, too. We might become insensitive—unaware of, and indifferent to, the feelings and needs of other people. We may lack compassion—be unable to feel other people's feelings along with them, to be sad when they are sad, glad when they are glad, and frightened when they are frightened. We may become ungenerous, grasping, holding our money, our time, our energy to ourselves instead of spending them for others, keeping them ready for our own goals. We can come to be easily offended, and when we are offended, unforgiving, magnifying small slights and nursing grudges.

We can see in this description of narcissism the opposite of intimacy. A narcissistic person is basically one who does not love, one whose will towards other people is not altruistic or benevolent but self-seeking and possessive, exploiting and manipulating, perhaps even willing to hurt or destroy others in order to get what he wants for himself. In psychological terms, such a person is a game-player. He does not take part in any open and honest exchange of selves with other people, but instead conceals his true thoughts and feelings in order to manipulate others into giving him what he wants. He is a defensive person, afraid to let others see his true self, afraid to ask for comfort and affection when he needs them because such a request would make him vulnerable, would cause him to give up his control of other people. And control is what he lives by.

Narcissistic people, in a word, are isolated people, people who do not live in warm closeness with others who feel a loving concern for their well-being, but in a cold, distant, and unapproachable loneliness. Psychologists and psychiatrists see such narcissism as a sign of mental and emotional disorder, of either simple immaturity or a more serious form of mental or emotional illness. Its extreme forms are seen in some kinds of schizophrenia and in autistic children. In fact, our word *autistic* is derived from the Greek word for *self.* The Greeks had another good word for one who lives a private, isolated life rather than taking full part in the community. Such a person was called *idiotes*—the root of our word *idiot.* He was stupid, not living the kind of life that is natural to a human being, frustrating his own deepest needs rather than fulfilling them.

Catholic theologians have recently identified narcissism with sin, intimacy with grace, and the process of moving out of narcissism into intimacy with the process of redemption. In this view, our narcissism not only makes us somewhat unhappy, unhealthy and immature. When it is our basic orientation, we are evil, sinful, headed for hell rather than heaven. And we are all somewhat narcissistic, because the deep and constant tendency to be narcissistic is the effect of original sin. Narcissism is thus what we most need to be redeemed from, by a gradual transformation in which we lose the traits of loneliness—our insensitivity, our lack of compassion and generosity, our inability to forgive. And that redeeming process literally transfigures us in the depths of our persons, bringing us into intimacy with each other and with the divine Intimacy.

Such redemption, or transfiguration, is the purpose of the sacramental life of the Church. Baptism initiates the process, giving us the pledge of those who are farther along in intimacy to help us in our own gradual transfiguration. The Eucharist is the meal in which we both celebrate the intimacy with Intimacy to which we are called, and receive the food and the intoxicating drink that move the process of transfiguration along. The Sacrament of Reconciliation restores us to intimacy after our lapses into narcissism. Confirmation brings us to an adult role in the community of those who seek intimacy with Intimacy, and brings us a special infusion of the Trinity that makes our adult intimacy possible. Holy Orders provide us with men empowered to heal narcissism by enacting the Eucharist and Reconciliation. Anointing of the sick heals the special tendency we have to become narcissistic in reaction to physical illness and the fear of death.

Our entire sacramental system, then, seeks to realize the fundamental sacrament, the Church, by healing our narcissism. The church must become a community of intimates who are intimate with Intimacy. And for that intimacy to come about, people have to be transfigured—we who are born narcissistic must be changed, must become warm, compassionate, generous, forgiving people. The sacraments are actions which both symbolize and cause that transfiguration. Matrimony causes it in a special way, through the power, the sheer redeeming power, of sexual intimacy.

The unifying of spouses is the basic result of sacramental lovemaking. The transfiguration of isolated individuals into intimate union comes about precisely by the spouses' making their sexual activity mean what it says—by living out, in every daily encounter, the total self-abandonment that occurs momentarily in orgasm. A man and woman who love each other, in every decision they make and in every action they undertake with a generous, self-forgetful concern for each other's personal goodness, will, indeed, over a period of years, find themselves transfigured. They will gradually but very deeply move out of the narcissism which characterizes the life of a private, isolated person and into a tender, compassionate and honest exchange of their very selves. Just as the best moments of making love will be orgasms that are neither his nor hers but theirs, so the rest of their lives will seek the personal good that is neither his nor hers but theirs—a single good.

They will not, for example, make decisions in terms of what promotes his career alone, or her personal development alone, nor even take turns at these. His career advancement will coincide with her personal development, for he will seek no career development that does not do that. And her personal development will coincide with his career advancement, because she will seek no personal development that does not do that. For each of them, anything that seems good for one but is detrimental to the other is not truly good for the one. Thus there is only one true good in every encounter—not his, or hers, but theirs. And in constantly seeking, and achieving, whatever is their common good, the two come to be one with each other. They gradually but truly cease to have private lives and private identities. They become intimate with each other, and, in that intimacy, with the Three who are intimates with each other.

This unification of spouses, however—their being two in one flesh—does not produce another isolated unit, a couple, or what the French refer to as an *égoisme à deux,* a paired selfishness. For sexuality, and human sexual intimacy, is fruitful. Sex, looked at purely as a biological event, is a mode of reproduction. That fact is our basis for distinguishing sexual plants and animals from asexual ones. Asexual organisms reproduce by fission, or budding, or some other process that requires only one individual for its completion. But sexual beings are different, precisely in their mode of reproduction; in sexual species, there are two kinds of individuals, who must collaborate in reproduction because each individual produces only one of the two kinds of germ cells needed to produce a new individual. Sexuality, then, is a mode of reproduction.

But *human* sexuality is not just that, not just a mechanism for bringing egg and sperm together so that a new individual may come to be. Human sexuality aims at the creation of human persons. Thus the sexual love of a matrimonial couple is fruitful; if the two did not wish to have children, and to have as many as they could nurture in intimacy, something would be lacking in their own intimacy. There is something lacking in our concern for a spouse's welfare if we do not include in that concern the person's ability to produce and nurture new intimates who otherwise would not exist. Thus we see the sacramentality of a couple's intimacy in its natural extension into their children and grandchildren, and so on into an indefinite future. The partners' sensitive, compassionate, generous and forgiving love for each other is also a sensitive, generous, compassionate and forgiving love for their descendants, beginning with the ones they directly produce and nurture. A Catholic family is thus a community of intimates with Intimacy.

The process of raising children is another genuine transfiguration, one in which children gradually learn the ways of intimacy and move out of the narcissism into which they are born. That process is an integral part of the parents' transfiguration, too. Children, in fact, make their parents grow up much more than parents make their children grow up. For there is no more effective school for learning self-giving love than the day-in, day-out care of those who are at first totally helpless and narcissistic, and require twenty or more years of generous, sensitive, forgiving and compassionate care in order to themselves become capable of intimacy.

But even family intimacy, even that which looks to the third and fourth generations and into an indefinite future, cannot, if it is genuine trinitarian intimacy, close itself off into a circle. For the God in whom we love each other, and whom we love in each other, is one God, indivisible and omnipresent. The love by which he gives himself to us in our family intimacy is one and the same love by which he calls everyone else. The Self he gives to us is the very same Self that he gives to everyone else. And so, just as we cannot truly love our spouse without also loving our spouse's family, and just as we cannot truly love our children without loving their spouses and their spouses' families, so we cannot truly love Father, Son and Spirit without also loving their friends and intimates.

St. Augustine once offered as an argument against incest that the circle of love must be widened as far as possible; thus we must choose as our spouse a stranger, someone not yet included in the circle of intimates that constitutes our family of origin. His argument is easily extended. God wishes intimacy with all of mankind. Hence in our intimacy with God we must wish that, too. We cannot logically exclude any human being, past, present, or future, from the sensitive, compassionate, generous and forgiving love that characterizes intimacy. It is in this apostolic aspect of sacramental sexual intimacy that we begin to see the depth of the redemptive process that each of us needs—and that true matrimonial intimacy effectively brings about.

Some recent sociological studies show that the main factor for children's persevering in adult life in the Catholic faith instilled into them by their parents during their childhood is the intimacy that they perceive in their parents. In studying adults who did continue to be Catholics and those who did not, the only significant difference was the degree of intimacy that the people studied perceived between their parents during the years of their growing up. The perception of the intimacy was what counted: if it was there but not evident to the children, they were not inclined to continue to be believing Catholics after they left their parental home. If it was present and perceived, or even if they mistakenly perceived an intimacy that wasn't there, they were inclined to keep the faith. But the perception of intimacy between the parents was the key factor—more important than sending the children to Catholic schools, more important than family prayer, more important even than the parents' going regularly to Sunday Mass (Greeley, *The Denominational Society*, pp. 242–243). There is something revealed here about the power of intimacy, when it is perceived, to cause belief in the God who is love.

The process of love, then, generates a community of intimates with Intimacy. For by the mere fact of being concerned for the personal goodness of someone, I come into intimacy with that person. His or her good becomes my good, and in the possession of that common good, we are one with each other. When a Catholic couple thus love each other, and their children, and everyone they meet, and all of mankind, they build the Church, right then and there, in and through that love. The ecclesial reality is there, from the first moment of their making the personal welfare of others the object of their sensitive, compassionate, generous and forgiving love.

But there is still another aspect to ecclesial intimacy, in which matrimonial love is an equally effective cause in and through its symbolism. We are referring now to the attraction of converts, of people who are in and of the church not just by being loved in ways that they may not even be aware of, but in their own conscious and free choice to join the community of intimates with Intimacy in its full, outwardly and ritually expressed sacramental life.

For people to make such an act of faith, they must believe that God is love, and triune intimacy, and that his inner life is infused into us. They must believe that that infusion, which is grace, is their own redemption from sin and death. They must choose to undergo the process of transfiguration that occurs in our active participation in the sacramental life of the Church. They must seek to be baptized, and to participate in the Eucharist as the ritual meal that both celebrates and nurtures the life of grace. Now such decisions, such choices, cannot be made blindly; people have to be motivated to make them. In other words, one who chooses to become a Catholic must know what he is doing, and find it credible. From where does such motivation come? It can only come from people's experience, primarily their experience of other human beings, of Catholics living their lives in a way that is admirable and attractive, which they want to share because it is real, and good.

In the attraction of such converts, we find a fourth way in which the sacrament of matrimony builds the Church. To put it bluntly, if we had the sexiest marriages in town, we'd have more converts than we could handle. For there is a powerful attractiveness to spouses who are deeply and evidently and joyously in love, obviously delighted with each other sexually, exuberantly happy in their life with each other. We are not speaking now of the sheer attractiveness of sexual pleasure—that, certainly, is strong enough to rule many a person's life-choices. We are speaking, rather, of a special kind of credibility in which sexual desire and sexual pleasure are the dynamism of a transfiguration of persons. For most basically, what any convert needs is a reason to believe in the reality of love, to believe that—as John puts it—"God is love, and he who lives in love lives in God, and God lives in him" (1 Jn 4:16).

There is simply no more powerful experience in which people find love credible than the experience of knowing couples who obviously enjoy each other sexually, and in that enjoyment, and because of it, are sensitive, compassionate, generous and forgiving to those they meet. For there is a definite ratio in married life between sexual pleasure and benevolent love—the two vary directly. As one grows, so does the other. When either one declines, both do. Unless we place some barrier, some kind of repression, in its way, the natural law of matrimony is for sexual pleasure to continually grow, to become more intense as the years go by.

Early romance is not an adolescent illusion, a trap to lure us into a commitment that we then live out by an act of will after passion dies. It is, rather, the beginning of a powerful transformation that deepens with time. The make-up of the human person, the close, substantial unity between mind and body, makes the death of romance and of sexual passion a tragedy that ought not to happen, and that need not happen. For when we choose, or will, something wholeheartedly, that willing is not a disembodied, spiritual action—

it is psychosomatic, involving our emotions as well as our wills, our bodies as well as our souls. The unity of body and soul, of will and feelings, is nowhere more evident than in sexual love, where feelings are the most intense that we know.

It follows, then, that spouses whose sexual feelings are inhibited suffer a loss in their love and in their symbolizing of intimacy with Intimacy. Weakened symbols are also less effective sacramental causes. And so, inhibited sexual desire and inhibited sexual pleasure diminish the power of marital intimacy to transfigure spouses into the kind of persons who might draw converts into the Church. Couples who overcome inhibitions of their sexual desire and their sexual pleasure are warm-hearted, outgoing, generous, and forgiving. Their ever-growing charity brings them increasing sexual pleasure that deepens as the years go by. What could be more fun, or a more powerful magnet to draw people to the Church?

The psychology here is evident: sexual feeling, unless it is falsely inhibited, is a powerful force for transfiguring us, giving us the traits that are the mark of intimacy. Sexual inhibitions have their power, too; they hold us back from our transfiguration, giving us the traits of isolation and narcissism. The attractiveness of people who are appreciative of their own sexuality is not just a fact of psychology. It is the dynamism of a sacrament. Thus if we Catholics really allowed sexual desire to have its full power, if we were not afraid of self-abandon, the people we meet would know themselves to be loved, and in that knowledge would find credible the God who is love. A certain number of converts will always come into the Church for other reasons, but they will do so in spite of the sacrament of matrimony, not because of it. To the extent that we inhibit our sexuality, we inhibit the church-building power of matrimony. If, on the contrary, we allow our sexuality its full growth, people who know us will find our enthusiasm for life very attractive, and will be moved to join us in the communal life of the Church.

All men and women have to make a radical choice in their lives, to really believe in love, in loving and being loved, or not. In a very real way, accepting our full humanity is an act of faith. It is a drastic willingness to believe that we can love and be loved totally, not in terms of what we do and what is done to us, but in who we are and who our beloved is to us. God is love. If we do not believe in and personally experience being a lover and a beloved, then we truly have not accepted our vocation to be fully human and to go even beyond human capacity through grace to love and be loved by the triune God.

Without such a radical belief in the reality of love, we look for meaning elsewhere. We reduce ourselves to a nonreflective, passive way of life in which we are conditioned by our surroundings and by the herd. Our view of God is distorted and unattractive. We see him in terms of power and perfection rather than intimacy. We think of him not in terms of communion within the Trinity and with us, but in terms of authority. Love is truly the most divine experience in human life. But unless we have a strong experience of loving and being loved, we can never hope to approach the faintest glimmer of personal understanding of God in his inner nature. It is our capacity to love and to be loved that *makes* us most God-like. It is that capacity that most reflects him and that we are called to develop. When that is obscured, any intimate relationship with God becomes very difficult.

Unfortunately, our talk about Jesus coming, taking on our flesh, dying and rising from the dead, the whole story of salvation and redemption, is often in terms of *what* we are saved from rather than *to whom* we are called. Salvation is, however, our entrance into the very life of God himself. Our vocation in life is to become lovers. The tragedy is that too often we look upon salvation as a rescue from misery in this life and the next. But just as when we rescue a person from drowning, the real purpose is that person's future, so too Jesus was sent by the Father in order to call us to our future in intimacy with them. In other words, love is really the fulfillment of our creation.

Our basic choice is to proclaim love. We are to proclaim first and foremost God's love for himself within the Trinity; secondly, God's love for us; and thirdly, our love for God as expressed in our love for one another. That proclamation is life to the full. Without love we have mere survival. There is only one full life, the life of God, which is love. That life to which he has called us is not just a future one, after death, but present now. We are called to glory now. And when we are totally loving we experience the glory that is God's presence.

The most significant and the prime instance of the proclamation of the love that people are called to is the sacrament of matrimony.

Not everyone in the Church is called to this sacrament, but all the other calls need the modeling, witnessing and prophesying of the sacramental relationship of men and women with one another in the Church. The sacrament of matrimony (which is to say, couples who are causal symbols of love) empowers the other vocations to intimacy. Without matrimony as the primary witness to triune Love, other ways of life in the Church become ministries—services to peoples' needs rather than exchanging selves with them in intimacy. An important element, then, in the dynamic by which matrimony builds the Church is in being a credible symbol of intimacy, providing people with the experience of loving and being loved that makes the most radical choice of their lives possible. The causal symbolism of intimate couples makes it possible for people to believe in the reality of love, and of the God who is love.

We simply cannot understand, much less accept, God, unless we experience being lover and beloved. After all, Jesus, the fullness of God's revelation, is the expression of God's relationship with us, his Word. "God so loved the world that He sent His only begotten Son" (John 3:16). Because of our lack of belief in love, we easily translate the love of God into terms of an impersonal patronizing, a care for our needs rather than intimacy. We see it as being something that comes out of his personal responsiveness to himself alone rather than his desire for or responsiveness to us as persons. But desire for personal communion is the essential note of any true intimacy. Without the quality of personal desire, love is very likely going to fall back into that of distant good deeds rather than intimate belonging. Furthermore, personal desire is a necessary element of ecstasy, and the goal of love that we are commissioned to is ecstasy rather than serenity. We are, most of all, to enjoy each other's company. The love by which we help each other and meet each other's needs is only a means to an end. Its purpose is our exchange of our deepest selves, our enjoyment of each other's persons in passionate ecstasy.

Passionate ecstasy brings distinct persons into the closest unity— that is the heart of the marital symbol. And distinct persons in close unity is the nature of God, who is love. The mutual indwelling of Father, Son and Spirit is beyond anything we can imagine. Each is totally identical with divinity; each of the three is God, and yet there is only one God. Hence their unity with each other is perfect, beyond what we can grasp. No one of the three persons has any shred of identity that is *not* his union with the other two. The Father's total self is his relationship to, and love for, the Son and the Spirit: and their total selves are their relationships to, and love for, him and each other.

And yet, each of the three Persons has a uniqueness that is in no way weakened by or absorbed into his unity with the others. Their different identities are established by their intimacy rather than threatened by it. The Father is Father precisely in his total abandonment of himself to his Son and Spirit, and so on. The three divine persons have unity-in-distinctness *par excellence,* intimacy in its highest possible form.

Truly intimate couples bring people into the Church by witnessing to the inner life of God. For membership in the Church is a life, a life of not just imitating but participating in the very life of God. The Church is, then, really a community of intimates, of otherwise separate people whom the Spirit of love unites. Married couples produce the Church as a community of intimates. Even though no one ever observes them in the act of making love, their transfiguration has its effects on all who know them. They become credible symbols. Other people see that they have something, something that makes life deeply joyous and satisfying.

It is one of the fondest dreams of the human heart that love should be real, not just a romantic illusion, a bit of sentimental wishful thinking that we outgrow as we pass out of adolescence. It is also one of the deepest fears of the human heart that love might not be real, that where it seems to happen, it is only an illusion or, if real, at least not very durable. And yet it is central to Catholic belief that God is real—and God, the supreme reality, is love.

Love is thus not only real—it is more real than anything else we can name. As God the Creator, Love is the source of the reality of everything else. And that supreme reality, love that is divinely real, is poured forth into our hearts so that our love, too, is real. And it is everlasting. But our acceptance of the reality of love takes an act of faith, a free willingness to accept what we do not and cannot see.

In accepting invisible and intangible realities, we cannot rely on sheer will power. Being the body-soul composites that we are, we receive all our knowledge through our five senses. We cannot simply decide to believe in God; we need support for that belief from something that we can see or feel or hear. One little boy we know stated very well this need for sensory reassurance. He asked his mother one day whether God has hands. His mother replied that the answer to his question depended on which person he was referring to, for there are three persons in God. The Father, being spirit, has no hands; the Son, having become man, now has a resurrected bodily life in which he does indeed have hands; and the Spirit, being spirit, does not. To this bit of theology the four-year-old quickly replied, "I'll pick the one in the middle." That was his kind of God—and ours too.

It is the mission of married people, then, to incarnate trinitarian love in a symbol that is credible, to be imperfect persons living in an intimacy that makes the intimacy of perfect persons not only credible but attractive. Actually, if we stop to think about it, we all come to faith, and remain in it, not because of logical arguments for the existence of God and the like, but because we know some credible people—people whom we admire, respect, and enjoy. They are the kinds of persons they are because of their religious beliefs. And we wish, then, to share those beliefs. If we never had any experience of intimacy on the human level, we would find the idea of divine intimacy, and the sharing of divine intimacy with us, to be totally preposterous, incredible.

Witnessing to divine intimacy by living in human love is the mission of all baptized Christians. The witness of the sexual love of couples thus extends far beyond each family circle. For Catholic spouses, like all other baptized Catholics, have to love all mankind altruistically. Sexual love has to be apostolic, as apostolic as is the Church. Couples, precisely because of and by their sexual intimacy, must take part in the Church's concern for the well-being of all people. And in our age that participation means a whole-hearted concern for what are called social problems: the threat of nuclear war and the arms race, world poverty and hunger, racism, and consumerism. There is a close and direct connection between a global concern for peace and justice, and sexual intimacy in marriage. The connection is in the very nature of orgasm as a symbol/ cause of trinitarian intimacy.

In his analysis of the inner life of God as that is mirrored in the human love and intimacy that we experience directly, Richard of St. Victor points to the need of lover and beloved to share their mutual love with some third person, someone beloved to both. In God this third is another divine person, whose existence then closes the Trinity. For the Holy Spirit, being a divine and thus infinite person, is an adequate recipient of the mutual love of Father and Son. Their love need go no further in order to be perfect. Human love, however, cannot be thus closed on a single third person. True, spouses must love someone other than each other, lest they be locked in a jealous exclusiveness that defeats both the symbolism and the efficacious power of their love. Their love must be fruitful, extending beyond their immediate selves to their children. The fruitfulness of marriage is thus rooted in the very nature of love.

It is obvious enough that if one person loves another, he also loves that other's relatives and friends; and to love someone as a sexual partner is to love his children, for they are the fruit of his sexuality. We recognize it as a failure in someone's love for us when they reject our parents or children or friends—"Love me, love my dog." But for Catholics, every human being is a brother or sister, all of them needing and deserving to be loved with the generosity and self-forgetfulness that are the heart and soul of charity. We see, then, a connection between sexual intercourse, the enactment of self-giving love in a marriage, and concern for the well-being of starving babies in Uganda, of blacks in Harlem, of bombing victims in Hiroshima, of all people of all times and places.

A Catholic spouse, indeed, has to be concerned for people of the future—for example, in our conservation of the earth's resources. For we see future people as potential members of our community of intimates with Intimacy, the Church. Sacramental couples must care, then, about an end to the arms race and to world hunger and racism. For if we don't, we are denying the intrinsic symbolism and meaning of sexual intercourse.

Let us try to see that connection more clearly. It is based on the psychology of motivation—how our motives for the things we do can either build or destroy intimacy. The motive that makes sexual love sacramental logically extends love beyond one's spouse to all other people of the world, including the unborn of future generations. Our motives, or goals, are what we have in mind when we act, the ideals that determine the way we act; they are the real reasons why we act the way we do. Thus two different people may perform the same action outwardly but have different motives for doing so. And those different motives will determine the quality of what they do, making it good or evil. Motives will also affect the personal identities of the two people. And their motives will decide whether their action builds intimacy or destroys it.

Think, for example of two businessmen donating money to the Jerry Lewis telethon—one motivated by a sincere desire to help crippled children, the other seeking a tax write-off or some free advertising that will increase his profits. The first is acting out of altruistic love, identifying with crippled children, loving them as his other self. His donation is an act of altruistic love and creates a deep intimacy between him and the children he helps, even though they never meet face to face. That first businessman has an identity as a lover and—if he is a Catholic—as a member of that intimacy with Intimacy that is the Church. His donation builds the Church by bringing more people into the circle of love, and by deepening the love of some who are already in it, including himself.

The second businessman, however, motivated by a desire for profit, does a quite different thing, even though he might donate an equal amount of money and obtain the very same medical care for the same number of children. He is acting not out of altruistic love but out of utility or selfishness. He does not love the crippled children as his other self; he does not identify with them. (If he could get the same profits in some other way, he would do so. Profit is what he is really after.) His donation, then, creates no intimacy. He has no identity as a lover; he is, instead, a money-maker. If he is a Catholic, he is so in name only, for he does not participate in the intimacy which constitutes the Church; he contributes nothing to the building of the Church, either by extending the range of love that binds her members together, or by deepening any love that already exists in his own heart.

We see, then, the importance of our motives in what we do— they make us be who we are, give us our deepest identity as persons. They often determine what we do, as well as why we do it—our greedy businessman might not donate to the telethon if he could gain greater profits elsewhere, whereas the first businessman would do so even if his profits were reduced. Motives constitute the basic nature of our actions, so that actions that are similar outwardly can be very different when done for different motives.

The first man's act, in which he loves needy children by identifying with them, is implicitly a love for all of mankind, including those who are not yet born. For this man, loving these children for their sakes will include concern for their future, for the kind of world they must live in. He will want for them the greatest good their lives can provide; he will want them to enjoy the intimacy with Intimacy that constitutes the Church. He will thus want all the necessary conditions for that intimacy to come about—not just health for these crippled children, but sufficient food, water, medical care, housing, clothing, education, political freedom for all other people—for these people are the intimates whom he wants these crippled children to enjoy.

A person who is motivated by a desire to promote intimacy, then, excludes no one from his loving concern and identification. For to exclude any person from one's loving concern is to deny to that person his or her intimacy with the triune God. Really the rock-bottom basis for the apostolic range of the sexual love of a couple is the unity of God. The three Persons are one God, indivisible and present everywhere. It is logically impossible to wish trinitarian intimacy to one person and not wish it to another, to all others. (See Meehan, pp. 182–188.)

Thus people who do not identify, as far as possible, with every single human being, loving all with the altruistic love that generates intimacy, must examine their motives in regard to the people they do love and identify with. For when we do examine our motives, we might find that they are not altruistic, but selfish; that what seems outwardly to be generosity, which is charity, is really selfishness, which is sin. Someone who loves only his own family and friends, for example, doesn't really love them for their sakes. If he did, he would want for them the best possible fulfillment—intimacy with Intimacy, in the Church. And to wish them that intimacy requires him to love all other people, too, as actual or potential members of the Church.

If we do not wish that for everyone, it must be that we enjoy, associate with, and adhere to our own family and friends because they are pleasant to us, useful, comfortable. Our motivation is thus selfish. Our love for our loved ones is only apparently love; really, it is kind of self-seeking, and that defeats intimacy for us all. As Jesus said, even the pagans do that.

Here, then, we see the connection between sacramental sexuality and the passionate concern for social justice that is an important part of the edifying, Church-building power of the sacrament of matrimony. The kind of self-abandonment that intercourse bespeaks, the kind of identification of one's spouse as one's other self, and utter devotion of oneself to the spouse's well-being that is symbolized by orgasm, logically leads one to passionate concern for the well-being of everyone else in the world. To put it in another way, any failure to love anyone *other than* my spouse violates my sexual intimacy with my spouse; it indicates a selfish motivation on my part that contradicts the symbolism of our sexual ecstasy.

In thus being selfish or indifferent to anyone, past, present, or future, I make a futile attempt to divide what cannot be divided—the love of God, which is poured forth in all our hearts. Thus if I seek to have the Blessed Trinity, by saving grace, present in some people but not others, my attempt is futile and self-defeating. Such exclusionary love indicates a selfishness on my part that must make me wonder about my motivation even in loving my spouse. To the extent that that motivation is selfish, our copulating (we cannot call it love-making, because it really destroys love) is not a sacrament, not a causal symbol and symbolic cause of grace. It is rather a countersign, an outward act that does not conform to the inward reality. Far from enacting a sacrament, then, I would be enacting a blasphemy, a barrier to grace, a wall that would separate people rather than bringing them into the Church.

The sacramental symbolism of sexual intercourse also implies an attitude toward having children. Sacramental spouses want children instead of seeing them as a burden. They do not breed thoughtlessly, of course. But they want to produce as many little intimates as they can, within their physical, psychological and financial limits. This same love for children motivates their concern for what are called social justice issues. Spouses who make love with the only kind of motivation that can be sacramental—charity—will be passionately concerned for a just distribution of the world's goods to all the world's people. Such a couple will not live a kind of Manichaeism, which sees this world and our life in it as an evil to be minimized and ultimately escaped. That view is a heresy which has been condemned for centuries. But such a couple will also not live the consumerism which is characteristic of contemporary America, which makes material goods and comforts and financial security the top priorities.

Consumerism weighs children and social justice and intimacy on the same scale as new cars, expensive vacations, and the latest electronic gadgets. Life becomes a calculus, an effort to balance all of these as equal values. A consumer-minded couple will plan a house, a car, and two careers, and then figure how many children they want to fit into their lifestyle. That consumerism is, indeed, a kind of selfishness, that makes any intimacy, even with each other, impossible. For it is contrary to the very nature of sexual abandon. Ecstatic, passionate abandonment of self to each other leads sacramental spouses to see their sexual intimacy, and the sharing of it with children, as their absolutely first priority. Material goods are not equal values, to be balanced off in some calculus with intimacy. They are means to that intimacy. Intimacy comes first. And intimacy is established only by altruistic love for all mankind.

Thus does God's love extend itself—first to Son and Spirit, then, through the Incarnation, to all of mankind. The sexual love of sacramental couples reaches beyond spouse and family to further complete the loving mission of Christ. This is the incarnation in which we are all called to participate with Christ by our baptism, to form a circle of intimacy that is greater than marriage, family, home. In accepting our mission we join with the Lord who "looking round at those who were sitting in the circle about him said, 'Here are my mother and my brothers. Whoever does the will of God is my brother, my sister, my mother' " (Mark 3: 34–35).

CHAPTER V

NUPTIALIZING THE CHURCH

Our Scripture speaks in many places of a marital relationship between us and God; Yahweh is the husband of Israel, Jesus the Bridegroom of the Church. Of course nothing said of God, and thus nothing said of God's relationship to people, can be taken in the usual, literal sense of the terms used. Ordinary human language is simply inadequate to capture the divine reality. Scriptural authors use metaphors and comparisons that are not meant to be taken literally. Our Scripture, indeed, includes many different metaphors to express God's love for us: He is our Shepherd, our King, our Father, Vinekeeper, etc. But the marital metaphor is the most frequent one, the central and basic scriptural metaphor. Hence we must give it some attention, try to understand it as best we can. The metaphor is, first of all, personal—God does not relate to us as some impersonal form, or primal energy. He relates to us as persons do—with a mind and a loving will, looking to that unity-in-diversity that we call intimacy. And we are to relate to each other in the same way—as Jesus prayed at the Last Supper.

God's love for us, which is also the model of our love for each other, being marital, is also sexual in some important sense, though not one that leads him to copulate with his creatures, as in some pagan myths. But God's love for us is not mere friendship or parental love—it is nuptial. Now, what makes marriage different from every other personal relationship we can conceive of, including ordinary friendship, is that it is sexual. Thus there is some important and basic sense in which the love we all have for each other is also to be marital, which is to say sexual.

Obviously our Scripture is not recommending promiscuity, or suggesting that sexual intercourse needs to be the action by which any complete love between persons is enacted. *Sexual,* in other words, is not equivalent to *copulative.* Even for spouses, sexual intercourse is not the only, or the most frequent way in which they enact their love for each other. If it comes to be that, if copulating becomes isolated from a daily tenderness in all their other encounters, it soon ceases to be satisfying and can become irritating, boring, or even repulsive. What is central to marital love, even when it is not enacted in intercourse, is the intimacy of individuals who differ as much as two individual can, and yet enjoy a unity that is as inclusive as any unity can be. For spouses differ from each other more than friends of the same sex do; and yet, they share more of their lives with each other than people do in any other relationship.

What the marital metaphor in Scripture must mean, then, is that we are to love each other as God loves us, with a desire for the greatest possible unity-in-diversity. And since unity consists in two persons, the lover and beloved, possessing a good in common—that of the beloved, which the lover chooses to identify with—we are asked to care for each other's well-being with the maximum concern that we can muster. We are to identify with each other's personal goodness with as much breadth and depth as we can, promoting that goodness by loving service, and enjoying it in clear and steady contemplation when it comes about. Such deep love, bringing us into maximum unity with each other, also promotes our greatest possible diversity, because a lover always seeks to promote what is unique and distinctive about his beloved's goodness, rather than making the other his clone.

A sexual, passionate element is unavoidable in such loving, simply because we are sexual, passionate beings. We are not spirits trapped or housed in bodies, destined to gradually separate from them in order to become more spiritual. Our bodies, with their sexual and other passions, are our very selves. We don't *have* our bodies; we *are* our bodies. Hence all fully human love is sexual and passionate, a love in which the lover puts his whole self, including his sexuality and passions, at the service of his beloved, and seeks to promote the whole self of his beloved—including his beloved's sexuality and passion.

Such love need not aim at, or lead to, sexual intercourse. But any love that did not include sexual feelings would not be humanly whole, and hence would not be the perfect love that we Catholics are called to show to each other. It would not unite us as persons in our wholeness; it would not promote our distinctiveness in a complete way. Thus every encounter between two persons, even a simple "Good morning," must in some sense be an act of nuptial love; it must be sexual and passionate. If it is not—if sexual differences and sexual feelings are overlooked or suppressed—the encounter is not an act of the completely personal love we are to show each other. We must seek, in every action, to bring our entire (sexual) selves into communion with the entire (sexual) selves of the people we meet.

Of course we are not to be promiscuous. Sexual love is not the same as copulation. But sexuality is not to be repressed, either. We mean that there are many ways in which to enact sexual love other than intercourse. Our nuptial love for all we meet is our whole-hearted, passionate concern for, and enjoyment of, each person's distinctive goodness. Such marital love is what God extends to us, his people. Such marital love is what we are commanded to show for each other, as our way of accepting God's love for us. Such marital love is what constitutes the Church, what binds millions of people over the centuries into a unity that, while deeper and more complete than any other, fosters their distinctive individualities.

The Church is, in this sense, a marital intimacy. Members of the Church are to love each other with a marital love. If we don't, we simply do not belong to the Church. We may *go to* Church; but we do not have the grace, the participation in God's marital love, that constitutes the inner reality of the Church. We are merely a collection of separate individuals who occasionally gather in the same place at the same time, and go through the same outward actions.

This marital quality of Christian love has important implications for the structure of the Church. The Church is meant to be unlike any other human society or organization. Her structures cannot be legalistic or authoritarian, based on an objective, impersonal enforcement of regulations. Rather, canon law and the other guidelines derived from it ought to be guidelines for loving, and be lovingly carried out. Every decision of every ecclesiastical court, for example, ought to promote the intimacy of all—litigants with each other, lawyers and judges with each other and with litigants, and staff. All the decisions made in the Church, from setting up the curriculum in a seminary to selecting a bank for a rectory improvement loan, ought to be made in such a way as to promote intimacy—the intimacy of all involved, including janitors and typists, bankers and pastors, and those who sit in the pews.

Any group of Catholics ought to enact, and to be known for enacting, a constant passionate concern for each other's maximum personal well-being. Decisions about making and saving money, about getting things done efficiently, about any other goal and concern, must take second place to our overarching concern, the promotion of that intimacy that is the life of grace. Catholics, whose very life is nuptial, ought never to treat each other—or anyone else, for that matter—with a cold, mechanical objectivity. What would a wife think of a husband who could be coldly objective about her? What husband would feel warm and confronted, *loved*, if his wife treated him impartially, just like everyone else?

Walter Mondale, when Senator from Minnesota, once proposed a bill requiring a "family impact" study as a prerequisite to the passage of any bill in Congress—a study of how each proposed law would affect family life. In the Church, every decision made, every action taken, ought to be preceded by an "intimacy impact" study—an inquiry to make sure that the action would promote intimacy among all the persons concerned. If it would not, it ought not to be done, even if beneficial in other ways. Our main practical conclusion, then, from our understanding of matrimony as a sacrament of sexual intimacy, is that the Church herself needs to be more deeply nuptialized. For the love between Christ and the Church is a nuptial love, and the Church is the primordial sacrament of her Bridegroom's love.

We have seen matrimony in an ecclesial context. Let us now look at the Church in a matrimonial context, as the Bride of Christ. For she is meant to be an even more basic symbolic realization of trinitarian love than are her sacramental married couples. Thus her visible face—the visible, tangible, audible structures of the Church that people meet in their experience of her—ought to be nuptial. She ought to be an incarnation of love that is generous, tender, and passionate. We now wish to offer some concrete suggestions of ways in which the Church might appear, and might be, more marital than she is now. Her decision-making structures are so important, so fundamental, and so visible, that we treat those first and at some length.

In brief, we suggest a much more extensive role for married couples, precisely as couples, in the decision-making structures of the Church. At present the Church has, unfortunately, many of the earmarks of a secular bureaucracy. Her values often seem to be efficiency and objectivity, the predictability of a well-oiled machine. A community of intimates, however, particularly a community which is intimate with Intimacy, would not be so depersonalized. Nor would efficiency and objectivity be her highest priorities. Instead, a passionate commitment to the good of people, an ecstatic love going beyond rational calculations, would prevail. She would live—and show to the world—the intimacy, the belonging to one another, which symbolizes that God is love. Her ecstasy could not be contained on charts showing lines of authority.

Couples proclaim the gospel by their intimacy, which is a sacrament that builds the Church. But if this proclamation is to be loud and clear, audible and visible to those outside the Church, married couples must be included in church leadership and decision-making. We need, then, to restructure the Church in such a way as to allow the charisms of married couples to have an impact on ecclesial decisions. We need a genuine sharing of power with sacramental couples. But what is power? We are speaking here not of the authority or influence attached to various offices, the ability to control peoples' behavior through reward and punishment. We mean, rather, the right to make decisions that flow out of intimacy and lead to intimacy.

Such power cannot belong to an individual person; it is communal. Its purpose is to proclaim the gospel. But our notion of proclamation implies more than the verbal communication of a certain "objective" teaching. We mean providing the experience of the gospel in relationships which proclaim nonverbally what is verbally preached—as in the sacramentality of couples who have achieved a genuine sexual intimacy. The spousal relationship symbolizes and effects the love of God in and through the faith community. But a sacrament, as a symbol, must be visible in order to have its causal power. Matrimony, then, can build the Church, can exercise its sacramental power, only if couples become more visible, their intimacy more influential, at many levels in the institutional Church. That visibility and influence will require a much higher profile for sacramental couples, working within the community toward prudent decisions, than has been the case in the past.

What we have at the present time is an institutional Church whose decision-making structures, personnel, and procedures greatly resemble those of a secular bureaucracy. People are chosen for leadership not for any expertise in fostering intimacy, but for their various academic and professional qualifications. Procedures are objective and mechanical, aimed at an impersonal efficiency. All decision-making positions, through the entire hierarchy, are filled by celibates; married people have merely advisory positions, when they have any at all. And the married people who are in advisory positions are there not because they are married, and thus have some expertise in intimacy, but for having academic and professional credentials similar to those of the celibate clergy. Married couples as such, without professional credentials, are practically unheard of in the Church's decision-making structures, at any level. The Church, far from being an evident intimacy with Intimacy, thus appears to be quite similar to any secular, professionalized bureaucracy.

Married couples as couples, selected precisely for their expertise in intimacy, will never be in any leadership roles in the Church as long as we continue to follow the present professional system exclusively. As long as Church leadership is a job or career, a form of employment, it will be allotted to individuals, not to couples. We have unfortunately priced charisms out of the Church and replaced them with professional credentials. We restrict leadership in the Church to those with a high level of academic training. Such training is not to be despised—it is an important dimension of the Church; but it is only one dimension. The Spirit moves where he will. We need to allow the charisms of the Spirit into public prominence in church life. Talent, training, and charisms are all gifts from God; all must be allowed to serve intimacy. The neglect of the charisms distinct to married couples is a great loss. We cannot hire these, or train people to them. They are God's gifts, given like other charisms for the good of the whole Church.

In the present organization of the Church, all decisions, from the parish level to the Vatican (and at all steps in between), are made by celibates—religious, clerical, or lay. Married people are conspicuous by their absence. In fact, a person's marital status, let alone marital intimacy, is not even considered when leaders are chosen. We do not look upon couples as couples as having anything to offer. Marital intimacy is not even mentioned on job descriptions. We do not mean that couples are consciously and deliberately excluded as a policy. They just are not considered, except on those few occasions that directly concern family life. But even here, our definition of family is so narrow that even these exceptions are not significant. Families are the Church in miniature; the Church herself is a family, brothers and sisters united in the common life of the Spirit.

When a married person—not a couple, but a married individual—does have a job in the Church, a position of leadership, that person is not there as married, but as a professional. Being married, and being obviously successful at achieving marital intimacy, is not looked on as a qualification for influence in the Church. Instead, we look for much the same qualities that secular organizations look for. The credentials are much the same as for one seeking a job in government, business, or the academic world. Marital charisms—holiness, devotion, commitment, belonging, fidelity to a community, the empowerment of the Spirit—do not count toward decision-making power in the Church.

In fact, someone seeking a position in the Church on the basis of skills in fostering intimacy would not be understood by most of our present leadership. As a result, the Church's public face is almost entirely celibate. We are somewhat like a corporation in which all the leaders are fiscal experts: they establish the agenda and goals of their company; they make decisions in terms of their interests and life experiences. These fiscal experts know, somehow, that production is important, too. But they cannot even imagine that production-oriented people could have anything to say. Their questions and plans would be outside the mental world of the fiscal experts, and so they wouldn't be considered. It isn't hard to imagine what would become of such a corporation. It could hardly survive, would soon have no fiscal questions to resolve, for production would have ceased.

We are in a similar situation in the Church. While both celibate and married people are essential to the accuracy of the Church as a sacramental symbol, its leaders are all celibates. Celibates set the agenda and goals, and make decisions in terms of their life-experiences. The leaders know that married people are somehow important, but don't take them seriously as having something important to say.

The tragedy is even more fundamental. Couples, ignored because they do not have the accepted professional training, and their leaders, ignorant of the issues, directions, horizons and spirituality of couples, seem not to speak a common language. The leaders resemble those English-speakers who insist that everyone else learn English, that any other way of speaking be a "second" language, inferior to English. The language spoken in the Church, the one that should be everyone's first language, is that of celibacy. Couples and Church leaders often feel, when they do speak to each other, as if they need an interpreter. The Church is, in effect, and in public appearance, a professionals' Church—her goals, norms, values, and horizons set by a professional class.

Professionals should, of course, have a place in any important human institution, including the Church. But in the Church, their role should be advisory. For the Church really is not a corporation, or any other kind of secular organization. She is an intimacy. In a corporation, efficiency comes first, and intimacy, if it comes in at all, is incidental. But in the Body of Christ, it ought to be the other way around—intimacy first, and efficiency second, as a means to a deeper intimacy. And those whose expertise is precisely in fostering intimacy should have a decisive voice.

The deepest problem, though, is not celibates as such and their exclusive control of decision-making power. The deepest problem is the mentality of the ruling celibates, what we call, for want of a better term, a solitary or nonnuptial mindset. Since the Church is an intimacy, anyone who belongs to the Church, leader or not, married or not, has to have a nuptial frame of mind. That is, all Catholics, if we are to truly belong to the inner life of the Church, must love with the whole-hearted, passionate self-abandon that generates our intimacy with each other and with the triune God. That nuptial mindset can be found in celibates as well as married persons. It can be absent in many marriages, as well as in the lives of celibates.

Thus the mere fact of being a married couple does not automatically qualify people for decision-making roles in the Church. Neither does the fact of being a vowed celibate disqualify anyone.

The real issue is the orientation, the mindset, the motivation of those who are leaders and decision-makers in the Church. The orientation that qualifies one for ecclesiastical leadership is intimacy; the skills that constitute qualifications for roles of leadership are the skills of fostering intimacy. We have called this orientation, and these skills, *nuptial,* for two reasons. The first is that the Church is the Bride of Christ, and thus in some deep sense that is hard to describe, life in the Church—the love that generates intimacy—is a nuptial life, a nuptial love. The skills needed by any Catholic are the skills that promote the nuptial intimacy of Christ with the Church.

Secondly, we have called this requisite mindset, and these requisite skills, *nuptial* because married couples who are truly sacramental reveal that mindset, and possess those skills, in the clearest and most dramatic way. But they may be found as well in any celibate—indeed must be present in any celibate who is to be saved in the only way possible, through membership in the community that is the Church. Mother Theresa is one extremely clear instance of the nuptial mindset, and the nuptial skills, that we are speaking of. And very many married couples lack these—couples who have gone through a wedding ceremony, live in the same house, share a bed, have sexual intercourse regularly, but are married in name only because they have no intimacy. They are just congenial roommates.

Both celibates and couples who lack the nuptial mindset think of themselves—and others—as solitary individuals. They seek, in dealings with each other, an impersonal efficiency. They are impersonally objective and legalistic in making decisions. They worship competence as a mark of a person's worth. The nuptial mindset is the same in both married couples and celibates. It is not correct to say that marital love is sexual and celibate is not. All love must be humanly whole, must be sexual, because humanly whole persons are sexual. The nuptial meaning of the body that Pope John Paul II speaks of is not just found in the bodies of married people, but in every human body. Nor is the difference between marriage and celibacy a difference of degree, in which celibates are free to love more widely, while married folk must restrict their love to the small circle of spouse and family. All Catholics, married or not, must love all persons everywhere, including those of the future; they must be ready to give up their lives for anyone they meet, even a stranger.

The difference between marriage and celibacy is, rather, in the mode in which ardent, passionate, sexual love for every person is enacted. For we are all celibates, whether married or not. Some people—priests, for example—are celibates to everyone they meet. Others—married people—are celibates to everyone except their spouses. But all of us as baptized participants in that intimacy that is the Church are to have a nuptial love for everyone we meet. Those who have spouses enact that love in a special way with their mates— sexual intercourse, and the whole mode of life that supports that. Celibates—and that includes married people *vis-à-vis* everyone except their spouses—enact that love in countless other ways. But it is a marital, sexual love in all these cases, because it is a participation in the nuptial love by which God loves his people and Christ his Church.

But it is possible for married people to have a nonnuptial mentality, too. The mere fact of having gone through a wedding ceremony, and living in the same house, and sharing a bed, and enjoying regular sexual activity, does not make one a nuptial person. Many people continue the nonnuptial mindset that they had before they were married. Thus both married and unmarried people can have a bureaucratic, legalistic, objective, efficiency-minded, competence-worshipping set of values. And both married and celibate people can have a nuptial mindset, which looks to intimacy rather than efficiency in making decisions and carrying them out.

The basic problem in the Church, then, is not so much the giving of decision-making power predominantly to celibates, but the pervasiveness of the nonnuptial mindset, even among the married people who do have advisory positions. Hence the remedy would be— and this is our recommendation—not a simple replacement, on a large scale, of celibates by couples in the decision-making structures of the institutional Church, though that may be a necessary first step. The deeper remedy would be a conversion of heart so that all those who are in decision-making positions would have a nuptial mindset instead, would have the achievement of intimacy as their basic goal, and would have some skills in that achievement. Thus the presence of couples in leadership positions would be only a means to an end, namely, the presence of nuptial charisms in all decision-makers, whether married or celibate.

When we speak, then, of nuptializing the Church, we do not mean a simple replacement of celibate decision-makers by couples, for such a replacement might perpetuate the same nonnuptial mentality that we have now. What we would like to see eventually is the filling of all leadership roles by those persons, whether married or celibate, who have the nuptial mindset that makes the Church the Bride of Christ. As a first step, we seem to need a strong infusion of couples into the Church's decision-making structures in order to make the nuptial mindset more visible and powerful.

The hope is that the visibility of the nuptial mindset, the pervasiveness of a desire for intimacy as the motivation for making decisions, and the application of the skills of fostering intimacy on a grand scale might transform the Church. A visible, public presence of truly sacramental couples in the structures of the Church might lead to a change of heart for the whole Church. As of now, there seem to be more couples than celibates who have that mindset. But we hope that the day might come when celibates might be as nuptial-minded as those couples, when all the leaders of the Church might think in terms of intimacy, and live by its skills.

One step toward such a conversion is a redefinition of love, which we too often think of in terms of doing good deeds and meeting needs rather than an exchange of selves and a commitment to intimacy. Without doubt, good deeds, self-development, and service are important parts of the gospel message. But these are only means to an end, the exchange of our personhoods with each other. It is the work of Christ, and thus appropriate for the Church, to run service institutions—schools, hospitals, research institutes and so on. People need health care, education, and the supplying of their physical needs in order to love. But these institutions are only a means to an end. They must have an essential characteristic that sets them apart from secular hospitals, schools, and so on—intimacy.

We Catholics must not seek to provide health care, education, and so on, for their own sakes, nor for the sake of profit or for better participation in the goods of our secular, consumerist society. We who provide services must do so as a means of fostering the intimacy that is our salvation. More importantly, we must live in intimacy as we provide those services. We simply miss the point of our lives if we make efficient ministry the end-all and be-all of our professional services. The mentality that we are calling nonnuptial—an impersonal concern for efficiency—believes that if everything is done correctly in service to the poor, the sick, and the provision of correct liturgical and other sacramental rites, then the Church will exist. But she will not.

Intimacy does not come about through outward rituals, dogma, laws, and an individualistic piety. We are wrong if we believe that these forces can build a community. Only intimacy, accepted as a gift of God and chosen as a way of life—a nuptial mindset—can build the Church. She is not a bureau of health, education, and welfare in which interchangeable individuals fulfill roles in a mechanical, impersonal fashion. She is a community of those who, through intimacy with each other, live in intimacy with the triune God. A high profile for sacramental couples in the Church would be a powerful way to replace the impersonal, nonnuptial mindset with that of the Bride of Christ.

Up until now, official pastoral authority in the Church has been structured through canonical jurisdiction, localized in pastors who are assigned to geographical parishes by their bishops. These pastors then preside over the liturgy for their parishioners. Now the boundaries of function in a parish ought to be clear. All should know who is canonically "in charge," just as in a family it should be clear who are the parents and who the children. But in a community of intimates—a family or a parish—there should be emotional contact, passionate love, across that boundary. The boundary should not be what is called, in the school of family systems therapy, a "rigid" boundary. (Cf. Minuchin, *Families and Family Therapy*, pp. 53–56.)

In a parish, such emotional contact would allow the people to participate in the decisions that affect the parish. Here is one role for sacramental couples, who are the ongoing ministers of their sacrament. A wedding, officially witnessed by a priest, is a kind of ordination, an entrance into a permanent way of life that is meant to serve the entire community. But pastors need to provide structures by which couples can exercise their responsibility, precisely by giving a voice to nuptial intimacy in decision-making on the parish level.

We might wonder what this voice might be, what some concrete instances of it are. What contributions could couples as couples make—not just to parishes, but also to diocesan personnel boards, councils of religious congregations, as advisors to bishops and directors of religious education? If we view them as accountants, lawyers, or teachers, their role is obvious. But apart from these professional competencies, what would couples have to offer? Such wondering is a sign of the conversion of heart that we need. We are so accustomed to looking for competencies rather than charisms, that we can scarcely imagine doing things the other way around. But we can offer a few suggestions.

One skill that sacramental couples develop is in the area of conflict-resolution. After all, sexual intimacy does not come in a moment, as a wedding gift. It is an interpersonal achievement, won over a period of years, through cooperation with the Spirit. That skill is developed through resolving conflicts, deliberately maintaining empathy, valuing differences. The Church needs to experience this paradigm over and over again, for conflict-resolution is an essential part of achieving any other intimacy in the Church, including that between pastor and congregation. The intimacy that enables couples to grow precisely through the resolution of their conflicts can show a pastor how to maintain his love for his people, and theirs for him, in spite of anxieties, resentments, and other negative feelings. It can show him how to negotiate issues with his parishioners in a way that affirms all the people involved, clearly, justly, and with love. The skills of conflict-resolution, essential to any intimate community, would have many applications if couples were given the visible role in parish life that their sacrament calls for.

Healing is another area in which the charisms of matrimony could help to bring about the intimacy that constitutes the Church. We have fine hospitals, to be sure. But most of the healing we need in the Church is not physical, but interior. There are many scars of minds and hearts, wounds that need to be healed. These are most often inflicted by husbands or wives, children and parents, other people in the Church. Indeed, the deepest hurts come from those with whom we are most intimate—we feel these more deeply, and they last longer than any other. But the healing of such hurts is a distinctive charism of the sacrament of matrimony. Sacramental couples are the ones most experienced in healing these. They become mature through reconciling with their families of origin.

Indeed, no couple can come to any significant intimacy without experiencing such hurts and acquiring the skills to heal them. One prominent need for such healing is in the current relationships between men and women in the Church, especially priests and nuns. Many women are angry at clerics and feel betrayed and used by them. Many clerics are distrustful of women. Priest-nun interactions are often power struggles that leave their losers hurt and resentful. Now it takes something more than simple justice to heal these wounded relationships. We need to replace power struggles with a mutual search for intimacy, a genuine sexual intimacy. Who better than sacramental couples could show the way to healing these intersexual hurts, to show men and women not just how to be fair to each other, but to give and receive passionate, ecstatic love for each other's very selves?

In sacramental couples, men and women really do love each other that way. And in so doing, they find their persons transformed, transfigured, redeemed. Married men can give clear witness to the fact that men who associate with women need be neither threatened nor placating, but can actually enjoy women. Married women can give clear witness to the fact that women who love men can give up their anger and reach out in joyful embrace rather than seeking to win and control. Married couples could have an important role as advisors to priests' senates, sisters' senates, provincial and diocesan councils, precisely in reconciling and healing intersexual hurts.

Giving decision-making power to sacramental couples would also help Catholic schools, from kindergarten through university. Rather than appointing people of professional competence (usually financial) to their boards, schools would benefit from the nonprofessional perspective of couples. Catholic schools have become deeply professionalized in the past twenty years, to the detriment of preparing their students for their distinctive life in the Church. We prepare them very well for a life in their secular society, but not for intimacy. We let norms and principles from outside the Church guide our decisions about personnel, curriculum, and textbooks.

We are not referring now to those schools that, once owned by religious orders, have been sold, given over to lay control, and ceased to call themselves Catholic schools. We are referring to a more subtle kind of secularizing in schools that still call themselves Catholic, and are under Catholic ownership, but adopt nearly all their goals and their curricula from secular schools, thus becoming in reality secular training schools. For example, we have many ecclesiastical disasters such as large universities training thousands of students to be competent engineers, journalists, businessmen and health-care givers. But their students receive no instruction in the skills of intimacy. They have no courses on family life, no sex education, no training in communication and conflict-resolution, in psychological growth, and the dynamics of interpersonal relationships. Moreover, the students experience little or no intimacy in their daily life in such institutions.

The remedy for this kind of secularization is to make intimacy the main goal and purpose of all Catholic schools at all levels, rather than the academic competence that mimics secular schools. Academic competence would not be neglected, but would be sought as a means to intimacy. That revision of goals would be helped greatly if sacramental couples, precisely as couples, had a strong voice in the decision-making structures of Catholic schools. In fact, those whose expertise is in intimacy are the logical ones to make decisions in our schools.

We are fond of telling the government, when we seek tuition credits, that parents are the prime educators of their children. They have a right, we say, to choose the schools their children attend. But then they have an equal right to determine personnel, curriculum, and textbooks. Of course they need to consult professionals, even delegate some decision-making authority to them. But the professionals should not have the only, the determinative, the final voice. Parents should—sacramental couples whose commitment is to intimacy above all, who respect professional competence but see it as a means to an end. Since the Church is a community of intimates, her schools must be such communities, too. Academic goals are important, but unless these are a means to intimacy, intimacy with each other and with our triune God, our schools are not Catholic. Couples who see everything—absolutely everything—as a means to intimacy are, then, the ones who ought to guide the decision-making in our schools.

One of the most crucial roles in building the Church as a community of intimates is the formation of priests and their assignment to pastoral work. Currently, Roman Catholic seminarians spend four years in full-time schools of theology. They are ordained to the diaconate in the third year, serve an internship in a parish for a few months, and are ordained at about the same time that they graduate with an M. Div. degree. Their spirituality is basically one of withdrawal from the world. Emphasis is on classroom instruction, library study, liturgy, private spiritual direction, and personal prayer. The formation of priests, in other words, has taken on the same characteristics of impersonal academic competence that we mentioned earlier.

Priests-in-training are out of touch, by and large, with the parishioners who are to be their future intimates. Seminary faculty and administrators make their decisions on an academic basis. Lay persons on the faculty are hired for their professional credentials, and since their jobs depend on their acceptance by the administrators, they rarely risk any criticism of the system. Many seminaries tend to overemphasize academic skills to the point that a kind of abstractive, intellectual competence takes priority over intimacy as their goal. Even in-the-field training sends men out as ministers, not as potential intimates of the people they serve. They are offering their professional and academic talents to those who lack these.

Who better than sacramental couples could help to heal such a reversal of priorities? Such couples ought to be directly involved in running seminaries, in making decisions about personnel, curriculum, and textbooks. Such couples, knowing from experience what pastoral skills they need from priests, should help to plan the non-academic part of seminary training. We tend to think that married people don't know about such matters, and would only waste time or even make things worse. But that assumption merely shows how wide the split has become between the two mentalities in the Church, the nuptial and the nonnuptial.

We do not mean to reduce the intellectual competence of priests, or the training necessary for them to acquire that. We are asking, instead, that it be put at the service of intimacy, that the fostering of intimacy be the prime goal of seminary education as it is of the Church herself. The source of priestly vocations, after all, is not the direct inspiration of individuals by God. Vocations come from and through the Church. As it is now, we look upon priestly and religious life as the turf of those already in them. We let clerics define their lives, and define us as the recipients of their services. But we the people of God are to form the Church as a community of intimates, and thus have a right to be involved in the selection and training of our pastors.

Those who understand intimacy are the best guides as to ways of producing the skills that pastors need for that purpose. Being the passive recipients of patronizing care is not our way to salvation, either. In fact, two of the most successful movements in the Church, the charismatic movement and Marriage Encounter, have given over the task of calling forth their leaders to the community as a whole. Neither of these movements would accept a volunteer to lead them, nor hire full-time professionals for that purpose. The communities discern and call forth their leaders; those who recognize intimacy and have it as their primary goal decide who shall go on for training that will facilitate the intimacy of all. We should follow the same procedure throughout the Church, for if she is truly to be the fundamental sacrament of her Lord, the charisms of intimacy must be more evident in her public face.

We are not speaking merely from the point of view of social justice, of people having been deprived of certain right by unjust structures. Thus it will not do simply to recruit couples into the present decision-making structures. We are not recommending that we recruit married people, and then send them off for some sort of professional training, so that they will act out of the same nonnuptial mindset that predominates in the Church now. We are asking something much deeper, that couples be allowed to function as the sacrament of matrimony. Truly sacramental, nuptial-minded couples will not fit into present structures. A gnostic bent, our lack of a truly incarnational spirituality, makes that impossible. The focus on good deeds rather than relationships, on ministry rather than intimacy, is not compatible with a nuptial mentality.

Rather than forcing sacramental couples into an impersonal structure, then, we are asking that couples be allowed to incarnationalize our thinking. The Incarnation has always been difficult for the Church. The theology has been developing for two thousand years, but we still struggle with the notion of a fleshed God in everyday life. We find it difficult to accept flesh as being spiritual in any way. But couples who achieve a genuine sexual intimacy do not find this concept so difficult. They can, in fact, be its credible symbols.

The true structures of the Church, then, are the structures of marital intimacy. In order to bring about such structures, to make the Church the community of intimates that is the Bride of Christ, we need a deep conversion of heart, a replacing of a nonnuptial mentality with a nuptial one. And one very effective way to bring about that change of heart would seem to be to give truly sacramental couples a more visible place, a more audible voice, in the decision-making processes throughout the Church.

As an example of what we have in mind, we would like to cite a couple whom three of the authors of this book met during a workshop on marital spirituality, in which we tried out some of the ideas of this book on an audience that included couples, priests, nuns. After the talk on sexual intercourse as a causal symbol and symbolic cause of the intimacy which brings us into intimacy with the Trinity, Bob and Rosemary came up to tell us that the talk had struck them as the voice of the Spirit. After about fifteen years of seriously trying to live the generous tender and passionate love that generates sexual intimacy, they had found themselves on a sort of plateau. Both felt that God was asking something more, something new, of them, but they had not been able to discern what it was. After our session on sexual love as a sacrament of trinitarian intimacy, they had their solution: they would start a second family. (They already had two children, ages 9 and 13.)

Exactly one year later, we received a letter, and baptismal pictures, of their new baby. The letter said, in part:

> Last year we took part in [your] Matrimonial Spirituality workshop. It has had an impact on our lives and changed them all around—for the better. After one of the sessions, we came up to you and told you how what you had had to say in your presentation had meant so much to us (had really spoken to our hearts, like water to thirsting souls) and we were now thinking of having another child. We have a boy almost 14 and a girl 10. You were very gracious and attentive to what we had to say. You were very supportive.

> Well, this one's for you! Let us introduce you to Mary Therese. We are enclosing several pictures taken the morning of her Baptism, September 8—the feast of the Birth of Mary. She was baptized at an all-school Mass with our children and all of the school children celebrating the event and praying and singing their hearts out in praise of the Lord. As I had been going to

daily Mass before and during my pregnancy, all the school children had been so excited about the stages of the pregnancy and were always inquiring as to my health and so looking forward to the baby's arrival.

Mary is so special and so loved. When we were trying to conceive her, we both went to the Sacrament of Reconciliation and tried to stay in the state of grace and prayed especially hard during this period. I think you can see that when you look into Mary's eyes—there is a clarity and purity there. Perhaps it is my imagination, but other people see it, too, and it seems to reassure them of God's love and faithfulness. Her smile is filled with so much joy and love!

We are grateful to God for Mary. We are grateful to you, too, for being God's messenger and prophet. Although our time together was short, it was meaningful. We will always remember you and pray for you.

Our talk on sexual intimacy had not included anything about having children; the decision to do that was Bob and Rosemary's, and another couple might well decide on some other way to deepen their sexual intimacy and make it a more visible sacrament in the Church. But the basic themes of this letter are precisely the themes of this book. Bob and Rosemary have a truly unusual degree of intimacy, of sharing each other's selves. They have a common prayer life, which is the height of matrimonial intimacy. They clearly intend their love-making, in its context of daily generosity and tenderness, as a means of communion with Father, Son, and Spirit.

Bob and Rosemary did not come easily to such intimacy. If we were to hear the full story of their life together, we would hear of many conflicts resolved, many confrontations, many healings, of *often* having to say "I'm sorry." We would hear of many decisions that sacrificed some material possession they might have enjoyed in order to give top priority of time and money to their intimacy. Moreover, Bob and Rosemary clearly see their intimacy as sacramental, as meant to be a sign to the whole Church of God's generous, tender and faithful love for us.

Such couples could be of very great help in the decisions that have to be made in the institutional Church. Their voice, the voice of sexual intimacy, should be heard loud and clear on parish councils, on school boards, on diocesan personnel boards, and in matrimonial courts.

In clearly revealing to the rest of us the difference between a nuptial and a nonnuptial mentality, such couples could bring about a true renewal of the Church, a change of hearts. Then, as we all became more oriented toward our intimacy with each other and with our triune God, the Church herself would be transfigured, taking on the adornment of a bride awaiting her divine Bridegroom.

CHAPTER VI

PREPARING TO
NUPTIALIZE THE CHURCH

Come with me:

I feel a special presence
When I'm with you.

Love with me:

God calls us both to join and
Face life anew.
Here with our friends and family
God seals our marriage.
Our water turns to wine
Through God's love.
Each day our love will deepen,
   if we remember
God dwells within our love—
Our life reveals God's love.

Live with me:

I love you deeply and
Devote myself to you; so

Come with me, and
*Love with me.**

*This wedding song was composed by P. Wilczak in celebration of the sacrament of matrimony between Patricia Swiatek and Richard Thomann, June 14, 1980.

The Church will become nuptialized—which is to say, she will become the community of intimates with Intimacy that she is meant to be—through the sacramental lives of married couples and of celibates. Sacramental couples will exercise their ministry by being dramatically clear symbols of persons who enjoy the greatest possible human unity-in-distinctness. Both kinds of people will have what we have called a nuptial mindset. The ceremonies of wedding and of priestly ordination will be ceremonies of official commissioning of people to these two ministries. But such commissioning calls for very careful preparation. We have long had in the Church what has been called "marriage preparation." And we've also had a formal course of training, seminary education, to prepare young men for ordination to the priesthood. But if we are to take seriously the role of sexual intimacy as a force for building up the Church, and pastoral ministry as serving the sexual intimacy of couples precisely through a celibate expression of the nuptial mentality, both marriage preparation and seminary training need to be changed.

Marriage prepararation focuses, typically, on two important ideas: that all the ceremonial actions have to be performed correctly, and that couples need to be warned of all the dangers and pitfalls that lie ahead so that they can avoid a divorce. Seminary training, even with some of the improvements that have been made since the Second Vatican Council, also has two basic deficiencies. Its spirituality is by and large one of withdrawal from the world, and the training looks primarily to an intellectual, academic competence. We would like, then, to suggest several concrete changes in the ways of preparing those who are to nuptialize the Church, whether through their marital intimacy or through their celibate witness to the intimacy with Intimacy which is our salvation.

A reform of the usual marriage preparation would have two aims: to encourage the ever-deepening sexual intimacy of couples that constitutes their sacramental symbol, and to emphasize the positive view of such intimacy that makes any warnings about divorce irrelevant. Who could even think of separating from one who has become "bone of my bone and flesh of my flesh"? As St. Paul puts it, a man doesn't hate his own body (Eph. 5:29). One way to bring about this reform is to give engaged couples a mission in the Church that is a foretaste of the mission to which they will be sent on their wedding day. An engaged couple already has, in germinal form, the intimacy that the wedding ceremony will recognize and ritualize as a mission to the whole Church. Thus instead of looking at engaged couples, as we do now, as objects of ministry, needing care and warnings, we ought to emphasize their positive, active role in proclaiming the good news through their sexual love. Instead of warning them that they are about to embark on hazardous duty, we would then celebrate them as new apostles, with an important contribution to make to the Church.

Such positive preparation for marriage must begin, though, much earlier than our present marriage preparation. The dating customs of our culture are, in fact, not a promising way for entering the sacrament of matrimony. Much of our current dating is an exercise in intimacy-avoidance games. Young men and women pretend not to like each other when they do, for fear of "coming on too strong" and being rejected. They pretend to like each other when they don't, out of a fear of being left out of social activities designed for couples rather than groups. Much of the arranging of dates, and the activities on a date, aim at proving one's self-worth and acceptability, at maneuvering for each other's approval, rather than an honest and open exchange of selves which would be a true test of a given couple's prospects for a deep, life-long intimacy. Such customs foster pretence and manipulation—the narcissism that is deadly to intimacy.

Our first step, then, is to provide ways for young people to meet, and come to know each other, in circumstances that would foster a relaxed and honest exchange of selves. Such dating was clearly exemplified in the movie we mentioned earlier, *Ordinary People*. Conrad and Jeanine, while both feeling some awkwardness that is natural to adolescents, were able to talk to each other quite openly—not just about their likes and dislikes in music, and in bowling—but about their most serious fears. Conrad found that he could talk to Jeanine about his suicide attempt in a way that he could talk to no one else, including his parents. Jeanine did not hesitate to apologize for embarrassing him with her own insecurities.

The movie showed real hope that the two could come to a genuine trusting and generous love for each other if they continued to spend time together. No one would wish, of course, a return to the days of arranged marriages. But neither can we leave boy-girl relationships to chance, as we do now, and base them on the values of our culture. In our television and movies, in the isolation of adolescents in their age-segregated peer-group, we automatically encourage pairing on the basis of surface attractiveness and consumerist economics. We can hardly expect couples who become engaged on these grounds to suddenly reverse their values when they come to the rectory to schedule a wedding.

We also need to encourage Catholic marriages more often than we do, for when two people differ in their religious beliefs, one of two results is likely: either they will avoid conflict by not taking their religion very seriously, or they will find their religious differences a serious barrier to a free and relaxed exchange of selves. Either way, their intimacy will be lessened, which is to say that the accuracy of their sacramental symbol, and its power to transfigure them into credible symbols of Father, Son and Spirit, will be weakened. We do not mean to say, of course, that intimacy is possible only to spouses of the same religion, and certainly not that it is easy or automatic when both are Catholics.

Moreover, we do not intend to slight the importance of the ecumenical movement, and of the possible unity of Christians that might come about through mixed marriages. But much of what passes for ecumenism is a lessening rather than a deepening of spirituality, to the point that Catholics marrying non-Catholics are sometimes treated with great kindness and understanding, while those marrying Catholics are taken for granted. Without being bigoted or narrow-minded, however, we can proclaim the beauty of Catholic marriages, and their higher likelihood of being intimate. Such a positive affirmation of our own family, friends, and community need not be a putdown of anyone else.

We need to ask, too, whether in our desire to seek the lowest common denominator we present a view of marriage that almost anyone, Catholic or not, finds acceptable. In that case, prospective spouses of other faiths may not even have an opportunity to become Catholics, may not even be sincerely invited to do so. It may be that we are cheating them when we do not present the fullest possible picture of what is distinctively Catholic about the sacrament of matrimony—the view that sexual intimacy is a causal symbol, and symbolic cause, of our intimacy with Father, Son and Spirit. People have no chance to make a choice about a married life that will very powerfully lead them out of their egoism into an intense inner life with the God who is love if that option is never clearly offered to them.

Prospective spouses who are not Catholics might be as inspired to such faith as their Catholic partners if they were shown, with due emphasis, the difference between marriage—which even the pagans have—and the sacrament of matrimony. Much of our current marriage preparation could be given just as well by secular counsellors—psychologically and sociologically sound, perhaps, but a humanism rather than a proclamation of the gospel. Somehow young engaged people must be allowed to realize that they are called to real holiness, to real leadership in the Church, to a deep personal transfiguration, a life in a community—not just a placid and "successful" partnership.

Many couples are quite content with such mediocrity—granted. They are like the man who went to confession and, when the priest began to offer him some advice, said "I don't need any of that, Father, just absolve me." But many young couples do seek a surprisingly high level of spirituality. We need to support their sense of vocation, their excitement not just for themselves but for the Church. We ought to celebrate the coming-to-life of a new sacrament in the Church, and for the Church. Instead, we often dampen their enthusiasm by warning them of the pitfalls ahead, and of the sinfulness of divorce. The last thing in the world that couples in love want to hear about is preparing for difficulties. No wonder so many marriage preparation courses are met with a noticeable lack of enthusiasm!

Engaged couples are so full of the realization that they can love and be loved, so eager to shout that proclamation, so quick to put each other first, that they cannot even hear what is said to them about difficulties that may lie years in the future. Engagements are times of hope, and hope is not fostered by the attitude "it won't last." It will last if the couple deliberately cultivate their sexual desire for each other. The lasting quality of romance is not a foolish dream, but a very realistic expectation. We ought to celebrate that expectation, and the enthusiasm that is the mark of the presence of the Holy Spirit. An engaged couple, after all, have made a promise to marry. The love they feel, and the commitment they have already made to each other, are a reality, an intimacy, that will be formalized in the wedding ceremony. That reality, their sexual intimacy, is destined soon to be a symbolic cause of Christ's love for his Church, a symbol that will be effective in building that Church.

One way to celebrate the sexual intimacy of an engaged couple would be through a solemn betrothal ceremony, in which the couple would commit themselves to the community. (After all, their sacrament is not just for them; it is for all of us.) And the community would commit itself to the couple, as a life-support system for their sexual intimacy. (After all, they cannot maintain their romance alone.) Various members of the community could symbolically lay hands on them, and make their promises of support more concrete at a reception after the betrothal ceremony. Instead of warning engaged couples of the dangers ahead, we could promise them help for all the years to come. "If you're ever in a jam, here I am," in the words of the old song. "If you're ever up a tree, call on me. It's friendship."

By involving all the members of a parish in supporting the love of married couples, we could do much to relieve our shortage of personnel. Such support doesn't necessarily require professional training, certified marriage counselors with master's degrees. Sometimes peer counseling is the best kind of all. We could even set up a network of helping people among several parishes, so that the guardians of a given marriage (could we say its godparents?) could move away, as often happens in our mobile society, without the couple's losing their life-support system. Or the couple could move and immediately be accepted by other peer counsellors.

Peer counselling for the sake of promoting sacramental sexuality would be a very powerful and clear instance of the intimacy that is the mark of the followers of Jesus. Such sponsors of marriages, or godparents to them, would be much more than tutors or therapists; they would be prophets, voices of the Church speaking to couples of their sacramental role, the role to which their wedding ceremony commissions them.

Once officially betrothed and under the guidance of their sponsors, betrothed couples would need practical ways to exercise their ministry. We can suggest several of these. One is to invite them into schools—grammar schools, high schools, colleges—to share their love with the students and faculties. They need not talk about marriage, which they haven't experienced yet, but simply the experience of falling, and being, in love. The intimacy of a young romance is of a special kind, one that is rarely shared with other members of the Church community. It would strengthen the intimacy of the Church if an engaged man would simply tell people how falling in love took him out of himself and yet gave him a sense of being more, not less. An engaged woman might tell in a very concrete way how it feels to be so dramatically decentered, to be not just willing but eager to hand herself over to another person in trust.

A young engaged couple in the full and evident enthusiasm of their love are a most attractive symbol of the love in which two persons find their life by losing it, come to be truly themselves in their surrender to each other. The Church is a marital intimacy. We who are to love each other as brothers and sisters must love with our full humanity, which includes our sexual feelings. Since we are sexed beings, we can only know ourselves completely, and be ourselves completely, in our trusting love for people of the opposite sex. Who can better tell us what that is like than a young man who has just discovered himself as a man in his love for a woman, and a woman who has found her identity as a woman in her love for him?

An engaged couple might tell how they met and fell in love, how being in love changed their perceptions of themselves, their relationships with their parents, brothers and sisters. They could tell how their tastes and interests changed—really changed—in response to those of the person they are in love with. They might tell us to what extent this grace of God has made them more attentive to people, more patient and understanding, whether they have reconciled with anyone as a result of their new love. Lastly, they might share their religious experience, their increased awareness of God, closeness to him, gratitude to him, their ability to pray. Their hopes and plans for further growth in these same areas would also be inspiring.

Such talks by the engaged would bring to many people a dramatic and credible experience of grace. For falling in love is a grace, the grace of a vocation. People in love feel the power of that grace in a very dramatic way. For all of us, grace is meant to do what it does so evidently for young lovers—to work deep within us, shake us to our roots, overturn our perceptions of what is and what is not real, reverse our preoccupation with ourselves into a total fascination with others. And grace works in us, without us—as anyone who has been in love can tell. Falling in love is something that we do not, and cannot, choose to make happen. It seems like black magic. It is, instead, a conspiracy, a con-spiring of chemistry and the Holy Spirit. The attraction between a certain man and a certain woman is, indeed, inexplicable.

All human relationships are made in heaven, but marriages are proverbially so. For that old black magic is the result of a whole series of coincidences that need not have happened at all; yet, once they have happened, the romance seems so obvious and right that we can only attribute it to some power above us, Someone who knows better than we do what is good for us, and makes our meeting happen when we least expect it. Engaged couples can show the rest of us very clearly what it means to be a community of intimates, the Church—individual people joined together in love and dwelling in the three Persons who dwell in us.

And after that showing, the students and teachers whom an engaged couple visited could very well pray for the deepening of the love they have seen. Their prayer will show that they have a stake in the couple's continuing love, just as the couple has in them. People who are thus in communion with each other can do things they could never do alone, can be what they could never be alone—intimates. People who admit their dependence on each other, in trust and mutual support, become intimates by that very admission. They become the Church.

Engaged couples might speak to other audiences, too. They might well have their betrothal ceremony at a parish Mass, and let the story of their love be the homily. If that were to happen, older parishioners who had become cynical about the reality of lasting romance might find their faith in love renewed. Long-married couples whose sexual desire had declined might be inspired to rekindle it. Everyone in the parish, in fact, would be made to know that marriage is not a sacramental ritual for a couple, but that the couple is a sacrament for the whole Church.

The strengthening of the community's faith in love through love's revelation in the ministry of engaged couples has a reverse side. For young couples, no matter how much in love they are, and how convinced that their love will last and even grow, do see evidence all around them that many marriages do not last. Besides the ones that end in divorce, many marriages turn into a kind of cold war, in which the spouses do not break up or fight openly, but settle into a mediocre congeniality, living parallel lives that never really meet. And young couples know that such staid couples started out with the same enthusiasm and confidence that they now feel for their own romance. The deepest fear of the human heart, in other words—the fear that love is not real but only an illusion—lurks in the depths of their hearts, too.

Many of them are themselves the children of broken homes or unhappy marriages. There is a reverse ministry, then, of more experienced couples to the engaged. We ought to bring engaged couples into contact with truly sacramental couples who have experienced the deepening of sexual intimacy over the years, as a way of confirming their hope for themselves. Indeed, older couples whose sexual intimacy has lost some of its original excitement might then recall what they once were, their effervescence, their irresistibility to each other. If they have settled into a somewhat muted passion, they might find the courage to renew their own sexual desire. There is something about the experience of love, whenever and however it comes to us, that is contagious; it renews the trust that we need in order to become vulnerable to each other.

Somehow all of us, whether newly engaged, long married, or somewhere in between, need to make again and again that basic decision to trust in the reality of love. The decline of sexual passion in a marriage is often a kind of creeping mistrust; "I don't want to get excited about him; he is always letting me down." Or, "Anytime I feel a little enthusiasm about her, she takes advantage of me." And then we begin to hold back. But when we do experience people who obviously do love each other, as engaged and long-married couples might experience each other, we say to ourselves, "Well, yes—love is real, after all." And we find again the courage to renew the trust, the vulnerability, and sexual self-abandon that generate intimacy.

Such witnessing to the reality of love is, of course, the life-work of any Catholic. But engaged couples give such witness in a very distinctive way. Another outlet for their witness might be in leading penance services for married couples. Those who are still in the enthusiasm of young love could ask the married couples to examine their consciences on precisely what should be the main matter of confession for the married—their maintainence of their sexual desire. Spouses could examine their efforts to remain attractive to each other, to cultivate their enthusiasm for each other as special, unique persons. The engaged could thus make the visibility of their sexual love a gift to the Church in a public fashion that would deepen everybody's love.

In that service, the engaged couple could tell what they do to maintain their enthusiasm for each other. Married couples might welcome such a frank mention of sexual desire in a liturgical context, might welcome a chance to repent sacramentally of their failure to cultivate their sexual desire, and to make a firm and public purpose of amendment. Engaged couples have a special charism for being sexually attracted to each other in a very public way, without being ashamed. That charism could very appropriately lead the way to powerful and meaningful renewals of marital love, the sacrament that builds the Church.

Engaged couples could also be given a special mission to children. They could, for example, take First Communion classes out for a day of fun. Such a day would not aim at any formal teaching, but at the sheer power of loving persons being together in mutual delight. The result would not just be fun, but intimacy—the intimacy of the Church with Father, Son, and Spirit. Several other results might follow, as those who are preparing for two special moments of intimacy with God—First Communion and wedding—shared each other's selves.

For one, the engaged couple might catch some enthusiasm for the Eucharist, an enthusiasm that many priests now find lacking in the couples who come to them for wedding preparations. The engaged couple might also find, in themselves and in each other, a surprising need to care for, and delight in, children. They may have talked at length about parenthood in the abstract, but there is nothing that can make that so real as being with children in an atmosphere of simple enjoyment. Oftentimes those who have children talk only about the negative features, the difficulties and problems, the awesome burden of doing what is right. What makes the gospel message attractive, however, is not seeing it as necessary, or important, or correct, but as joyous. Personal joy makes love attractive. Children are attractive, and make parenthood attractive, when we are able to simply enjoy them.

This particular joy and enthusiasm flow in both directions, too. Engaged couples often find the excitement of their love dampened somewhat by the restraint of the adults they associate with. Their families and friends so easily take in stride this miracle which has happened to them, their grace of vocation. Older adults send them the rather glum message, "Well, there's nothing special about that. Besides, it won't last anyway."

Children don't have these chilling attitudes. They delight in knowing that any two people love each other; they make that love a topic of their excited conversation. They assume that romance is real, and it never occurs to them to think, "Aw, it won't last." Engaged couples, then, can find some genuine reinforcement from children that they might not get from the adults in their lives. Children are quick to feel enthusiasm, and are open in expressing it.

That open enthusiasm is not just pleasant for an engaged couple; it is crucial to the growth of their love. For the reluctance of adults to feel fully the joy of young romance, and to openly share that joy, is one of the common barriers to intimacy. Feelings commit us to each other; holding ourselves aloof, "playing it cool," is an intimacy-avoidance game. The confidence of a young couple in the reality of their love is an absolutely necessary condition for that love to grow. It can be either weakened or strengthened by other people's reactions to it.

The benefits to the First Communicants could be just as profound. The Eucharist is the sacrament of intimacy *par excellence,* in which Christ gives his very self to us, and we pledge our very selves to him. What better preparation for that eucharistic exchange of selves than the company of a couple who give themselves to each other in a very obvious and wholehearted way? When people are in love, they are at their best—their most tender, most patient, most generous. And it is those best selves that engaged couples share so freely. They are a kind of epitome of the enthusiastic intimacy that the Eucharist is meant to bring about. And they make that kind of intimacy most attractive. They help us all to realize what the Eucharist really says—that in order to be our best selves, we need not be talented, we need not be active, we need not be dutiful. We need only be there, being ourselves, sharing personal presence.

The motto of matrimony and of the Eucharist, too, is the opposite of the motto of the busy pragmatist. Instead of saying, "Don't just stand there, do something," we say, "Don't just do something—be there." Children who experience the joy of simple personal presence are ready to enjoy it in the Eucharist, and may take it home to their families, encouraging a new gentleness and responsiveness there. Their parents may be less afraid to let their own sexual intimacy grow and be more evident when they see such intimacy in an engaged couple having positive effects on their children.

This interchange between engaged couples and children preparing for first communion is an instance of the sacramentality of the Church. Sacraments become real when sacramental people come into intimacy with each other. Such intimacy radiates throughout the entire community. The engaged couple might become more loving, more gentle toward their brothers and sisters—with ramifications for the kind of parents that these young ones will someday be to their children. They might even inspire a new depth of sexual intimacy in their own parents, who would then become more credible symbols to all the people they meet. In the interactions of sacramental people, then, we can begin to see what the Church truly is—not the bureaucratic organization that her public face reveals, but the intimacy of a human community with the intimacy of God.

We can easily imagine other ministries that engaged couples might be sent to. They might visit, in order to share their love, with old people who are confined to their homes. Such visits would not just distract the old from their aches and pains for a short time, but would bring them the stimulation of life. Engaged couples might very appropriately seek a blessing, in whatever form, from old people who have lived lives of sacramental intimacy for many years. The motherhouses of religious orders, too, could benefit from, and give help to, young engaged couples. Again, the purpose would be that simple, joyous exchange of selves that is of the essence of intimacy. Many Catholic young people grow up without coming to know nuns, and nuns who live in motherhouses are often isolated from any experience of loving couples. Retired priests, often forgotten by those they once served, could also enjoy an outing, or other contacts with engaged couples.

In all of these cases, the engaged couples would be commissioned by their parish. But the object of their visits would be not so much a solemn formality as extending parish intimacy to those who might otherwise be excluded from it. A couple's sense of mission could also be strengthened by their adopting a foreign missionary to write to and support, from the beginning of their marriage. Such an ongoing contact with the foreign missions would be an excellent way to realize that marriage is not just for a couple, nor even for their family. It is for the whole Church. The sacramental power of sexual love depends very directly on the concern, the loving concern, that spouses have for every human person in the world.

There are several ways in which the wedding ceremony might be made more intimate, and thus an act of the love to which the Church calls a couple and for which she commissions them. As it is now, many contacts between various participants in the wedding are purely formal and impersonal, with no loving exchange of persons. We would think that weddings, above all, should be events marked by intimacy. Instead, we have—just as an example—witnesses who are scarcely known to the priest, and altar boys who are strangers to the couple.

One way to turn a wedding into a genuine exercise of ecclesial intimacy would be for the couple to develop some sort of personal relationship with the boys who will be their servers—perhaps have them to their homes for dinner, or take them on a day's outing. Altar boys, like most youth in our culture, are often overlooked and used as mere functionaries at many weddings. They ought to be, and be made to feel that they are, important participants in an exercise of intimacy in which they, too, come into intimacy with the three divine Persons.

The role of the Church's official witnesses—best man and maid or matron of honor—needs to be nuptialized, also. They are not meant to be merely a handsome fellow in a tuxedo who can come up with the ring at the appropriate moment, and a lovely woman in a special gown who signs the register after the ceremony. True, in most weddings these attendants are special friends of the bride and groom, are significant in their lives and can have great influence over them. What is missing, though, is their function as official witnesses of the Church, witnesses to the Church's calling of the couple to sexual intimacy as their ecclesial mission. Many attendants are not Catholic; many of those who are do not even meet the priest until the rehearsal the night before the wedding. Some sort of earlier dialogue would help these witnesses to see themselves as having a crucial role in supporting the ongoing intimacy of the newly married couple, on behalf of the Church.

They are assuming a responsibility similar to that of sponsors at baptism and confirmation, to support the couple in their efforts to grow in love—in the compassion, generosity and forgiveness that generate intimacy, all through their married years. Since intimacy is a process, not a momentary event on the wedding day, the responsibility of the official witnesses of the Church is an ongoing process, too. They personify, make concrete, the Church's promise to support the couple in the lifelong process of achieving sexual intimacy. There may be a problem from time to time with a bride and groom wishing to have attendants who do not understand this responsibility, do not wish to assume it, or are not even Catholics. In that case, they could still be the official, ceremonial witnesses, but other guardians of the sacrament could be appointed by the parish— preferably experienced couples who have developed some expertise in the fostering of sexual intimacy.

One beautiful way to assure the continuance of the intimacy of the wedding party after the ceremony would be for the couple to compose their own personal wedding prayer, to use throughout their married life, including a Scripture verse that will be the theme of their marriage. The prayer could be distributed to all the people at the wedding, with the request that they say it daily on the couple's behalf. The couple, in turn, would say the prayer together each day, in their quest for the particular virtues that they need in order to learn how to love. Such prayer, focusing very concretely on the relationships of all the people who say it each day, would be a powerful exercise of the evangelism of matrimony. In it, the loving concern of the couple goes beyond themselves, as they and those who have become their intimates through the wedding ceremony are united in prayer.

We can think of objections to these suggestions—that they are too idealistic, too time-consuming, that most couples would not be interested in making their wedding into such an exercise of ecclesial intimacy. Our reply to this objection is that the opportunity should be offered, for the sake of those who would welcome it. Even if one tenth of our weddings were of this type, they would have a great power to increase the love of those couples and to make them more accurate, and thus more effective, symbolic causes for all of us of intimacy with God. Another problem is that priests, deacons, and others involved in marriage preparation have no inclination, nor time, for this kind of involvement with wedding parties. A standard, depersonalized, routine format is so much easier to work with. In this objection, we see the nonnuptial mentality at work, the mindset that defeats intimacy in the Church.

The only solution to that problem is to change that mindset, to welcome couples with the enthusiasm that is due them as a sacrament that builds the Church that is the Bride of Christ. Do we believe in the reality of love, especially young romantic love, or don't we? If we do, then we must feel an urgency to make the most of its sacramental power. If romantic love is ever to be properly celebrated in the Church, weddings that are carefully prepared so as to be events of maximum intimacy are the time and place for its celebration.

The interaction that we recommend, between the spouses as ministers of the sacrament and the Church's official witness, is a clear instance of the inseparable connection between marital and priestly spiritualities, between wedded and celibate intimacy. Each is a side of the same coin, each unable to exist without the other. And the value of that coin is the love that credibly proclaims our discipleship with Christ, that is our intimacy with the triune God: "By this all men will know that you are my disciples, if you have love for one another" (John 13:35).

If we are to take seriously the sacramental power of matrimony— the transfiguration of couples into credible symbols who will attract others to believe in the God who is love—then we must also give some thought to the formation of priests, to ordination preparation. For here we can see some of the same deficiencies that mar our present marriage preparation, especially a kind of impersonal formalism that focuses on the rights and wrongs of the ordination ceremony, and a tendency to see ordination as an isolated, momentary event rather than a lifelong process of growing into ever deeper ecclesial intimacy. We offer, then, a few practical suggestions for improving seminary training.

Basically, seminarians need, first and foremost, to live lives of intimacy, and thus to learn its dynamics. In our contemporary society, such a spirituality for diocesan clergy would be something of a departure from the monastic spirituality that developed very early in the Church and became the dominant mode. At the present time, men are prepared for the priesthood in various diocesan, regional, and national seminaries. The formation is, of course, determined by the faculty and other staff members of these institutions, usually diocesan clergy and members of religious orders, with a few laymen included. The training is primarily intellectual and academic, with some field requirements added. Most often the seminaries are isolated geographically from the communities in which the future priests will do their life's work. And added to this isolation is a very important cultural factor that has a powerful effect, reinforcing the barriers to intimacy that are already present in an isolated academic institution. We are referring to the dwindling of community life to almost nothing.

There was a time when seminarians came out of ethnic neighborhoods that gave them strong ethnic and social identities before they were withdrawn for spiritual formation and pastoral training. Some seminaries even maintained this ethnic identity, and prepared their graduates to serve in identifiably Irish, German or other ethnic parishes. Such a situation almost required some sort of isolation for developing pastoral leadership; "Father" could not be viewed as "Just one of the guys." He had to have some distance from his people in order to make hard decisions and to challenge them. But despite the collar, he was one of them, known to them, accepted and followed by them. He was both distant and connected—that is, a member of their community. Such a communal background is no longer common in our society.

Today, many ethnic neighborhoods have been replaced by streets of disconnected residences. People occupy houses that are close to each other, but spend most of their significant hours elsewhere and often do not get to know each other. Neighbors do not know each other's names, families, hopes, sufferings, or values. Rather than being communities, such groups of people are assemblies of the alienated—"the lonely crowd." (Cf. Urie Bonfrenbrenner's *Two Worlds of Childhood*, pp. 95–97.) Such lack of community life distorts privacy—which is essential for the growth of intimacy—into isolation, which is intimacy's death. A seminary spirituality of withdrawal, once beneficial, is harmful in our present social situation, because it makes an already noncommunal way of life even worse. We need a renewal of seminary spirituality, through a renewal of seminary education, that will enhance and deepen the preparation for ministry while at the same time fostering intimacy in a lived community.

One specific step toward the intimacy-oriented seminary life would take us back to the spirit of the decree on seminary education of the Council of Trent, which ordered that seminaries be established in cathedral churches so that seminarians would serve as apprentices under more experienced pastors. The apprenticeship method of education teaches a future priest not so much the mechanics of a bureaucracy as a concern for the need of persons, through actual contact with people and through direct experience of the intimacy-fostering work of masters of the art. The training of medical students, with its heavy emphasis on clinical experience, is based on this principle. Medicine cannot be learned exclusively from lectures and textbooks—hence the association of medical schools with teaching hospitals. Our seminaries could do something similar, by making certain parishes "teaching parishes."

Thus, a seminarian, after a semester of traditional academic training and spiritual direction, could be assigned to five or ten households as his own "congregation." Under the supervision of the official pastor and of the appropriate seminary staff, he would serve these families as a pastoral apprentice, his households constituting a "neighborhood church." He would come to know every member of those households by name, and become familiar with their strengths and their needs. A spiritual director would help him to deepen his intimacy with his parishioners as the way to deepen his intimacy with God. A field education advisor would help him to correlate his ministry with his systematic study of theology and other academic disciplines. In the second and third years of his training, the seminarian—still a pastoral associate for the same "neighborhood church"—would come to know members of the extended families, thus experiencing the lives of a family over several generations.

Such a long contact with the same families would give him a depth of knowledge and compassion not possible in any other way. He would experience what it takes to be a loving person—generous, ecstatic, passionate—in marriages and births, illnesses and deaths, crises of psychological growth, conflicts, anxieties, joys and satisfactions. He would celebrate the spiritual import of those events, which is to say, he would enter directly into the process of building the intimacy that is the Church among his parishioners.

Such realistic training would not only help to prepare him for his future as one who fosters ecclesial intimacy; it would also help to counter some of the trends toward alienation that currently disrupt our society. The result would be a new identity for the seminarian— not that of a functionary in a bureaucratic machine, but that of a spiritual father. A father is one who unifies the diverse members of a household in order to foster their constant growth into deeper intimacy. But a father can scarcely be one who does not know his children by name, and is not known to them as a person.

We could expect such a reform of seminary education to attract vocations to the priesthood. Much of the disinterest in the priesthood now is surely due to an uncertainty about priestly identity. But to have young men directly experience, and know as intimate friends, pastors who show the passionate generous love that causes intimacy in everyday life ought to make that way of life more definable, and more attractive. Such a seminarian, the intimate of his people, would share with them his own hopes and fears, thus touching their hearts and drawing them into a passionate and generous love for him. Such seminarians would convey more eloquently than words ever could that the priestly life, with its celibate commitment to transcend biological fatherhood, is indeed a credible symbol of the God who is love.

Such a spiritual renewal in seminaries would transform parishes from institutions into communities. Such communities, with large numbers of married couples devoted to achieving the maximum sexual intimacy of which they are capable, would gladly follow the leadership of their celibate ministers, who would be equally credible symbols of the ecstatic love that is the inner life of God. The divorce rate would surely drop, not because people had a strong sense of duty or feared social disapproval, but because husbands and wives would experience the happiness of belonging to each other in a large community of intimates, all of whom belong joyously to each other. Freed of the need to find excitement, escape conflict and pain, search for a fulfilling identity, they would deepen their intimacy with each other. Such communities would clearly proclaim the good news that God is love, and we who live in love live in God, and he lives in us. The joy of such intimacy with God, an intimacy that saves us from sin and death, would be felt in the marriage beds of such a parish, and shouted from the rooftops by the lived vows of priests and religious.

Wouldn't such parishes be beacons of light to the world comparable to the monasteries in the dark ages? Where else will our spiritual values, and their cultural results, be preserved? There will be no other communities if the utilitarian spirit, which turns people into objects and which now rules our society, continues to prevail. A selfish manipulation of people for the sake of one's own fulfillment is the death of community as surely as were the barbarian hordes who overran the civilization of Rome. It may be up to parishes, to sacramental couples guided by loving pastors, to preserve the life of God in our world, as did the monasteries in the middle ages.

An old saying goes, "All the world loves a lover." That saying comes out of human experience, but it fits well with the basic message of Jesus, too. It tells us how sacramental symbolism works—in couples and in priests, but in all the other sacraments, too. When we meet someone who loves, who is a lover, we meet someone who is in the process of being transfigured. A lover is someone we can trust to be for us rather than against us, a person with a secure identity and self-esteem that free him from any need to manipulate us. Thus freed from our fears of being manipulated and used, we love the lover who frees us, and become lovers ourselves. Such is the dynamic of sacramental causality—love begets love by making love credible. Priests need to be trained in loving, in fostering intimacy, especially the sexual intimacy of the married, who are the majority of their parishioners. Married couples need to be helped to achieve their deepest possible sexual intimacy, to live the commission that they receive from the Church to build the Church.

These practical suggestions, aimed at making seminary life more intimate and intimate couples more apostolic, are only some of the ways that a new marital spirituality might be lived in the concrete reality of everyday life. In any case, we need to see that sacraments are not rites, or things, or abstract actions. Sacraments are persons, persons in community, persons who are intimate with each other and, in that very intimacy, intimate with Father, Son, and Spirit, who are intimates *par excellence*. Sacraments are the Church in communal action, then, for no one can be intimate, and thus sacramental, alone.

In a very true sense, matrimony is the key sacrament—a great sacrament, St. Paul called it. But the greatness of matrimony has scarcely been recognized. The sacrament was juridically defined more than 800 years ago. But it has not found its full place in the Church as yet. We need a marital spirituality in order to bring that about. But such is the life of the Church—she, too, is in a process, her lifelong process of becoming what she is meant to be, the Bride of Christ. One of the authors of this book was talking one day to one of the Bollandists—the Jesuit historians who are the world's greatest authorities on who has, and who has not, been recognized as a saint. When asked why there are so few canonized married saints, the quiet scholar replied, "I think we must admit in all simplicity that it has taken the Church a long time to realize that marriage is a sacrament."

EPILOGUE:
Transfiguration

When Jesus, before he went to his death, took bread and wine into his hands at the Last Supper and said: "Take, eat, this is my Body. . . . Take, drink, this is my Blood," he was proclaiming the power of his Spirit of love to transfigure simple bread and wine into his very own Body and Blood.

Christianity, as taught by Jesus and practiced by his followers, is a faith in the redemptive infusion of divine life within human existence. Jesus taught that new life did not come unless something else died. A seed of wheat had to fall into the earth and die before it could bring forth a hundredfold (John 12:24). He himself would die for mankind and be lifted up on the cross before he could draw all men to himself in his risen life.

The Eucharist is a microcosmic, sacramental action that not only signifies but also effects what it signifies, namely, that bread and wine under the power of the Holy Spirit become the "meeting place" for us to encounter Jesus Christ and his heavenly Father through the Spirit of love, as we are nourished by Jesus' Body and Blood.

In our oneness with Jesus Christ in the Eucharist we are brought into the inner life of the Trinity. Here is the climax of God's eternal plan, for he "chose us in Christ, to be holy and spotless, and to live through love in his presence" (Eph. 1:4). Sin impedes our being transfigured into Christ by love. But the Eucharist restores and powerfully builds up this oneness with Christ.

Marriage is a model of the transfiguration of the world. Spouses

157

communicate to each other the transforming power of the Spirit of love. They give each other the presence of the triune God. Their ministry brings about an intimacy that frees them to become their unique selves before God and before each other. Insofar as they receive the light of Christ in their conjugal union, however, they contribute to the transfiguration of the world around them as well.

THE TABORIC LIGHT

In the Christian East the feast of the Transfiguration on August 6 is celebrated with special solemnity, not only as a commemoration of Christ's transfiguration before his three disciples on the mount, but as a process that we Christians are also experiencing throughout our earthly lives. The first fruits of grapes, wheat, vegetables and other fruits and grains are brought to the church on this day, to be blessed and offered to God. The parishioners pray for a full harvest. But as they take home the blessed fruits of their long months of labor, bringing forth a harvest from seeds planted in the ground in early spring, or from vine and tree branches that had been carefully pruned, they enact in a symbolic way what is happening in their own spiritual lives.

In baptism the seeds of divine life were sown into our beings as we were consecrated by the indwelling Trinity to a life of growing into greater intimacy in the Body of Christ, the Church. Over the long years that make up the spring and summer of our lives, we mature, through many death-resurrection experiences, so that divine life leads us to the full harvest of our autumn years of life on this earth.

The feast enlivens our belief that what had always been in the man, Jesus Christ, burst forth in an anticipated vision for the three disciples, Peter, James and John, a vision of what they would later experience as the constant presence of the glorious, risen Jesus in their lives.

TRANSFORMING CONSCIOUSNESS

All Christians, married or not, are specially called by baptism to enter daily into that process of transformation that takes place in us as we surrender to the infinite light of the triune God dwelling in

us. The center and meaning of life will now no longer be in persons
or things outside of us, or, above all, in our own selfish beings, but
only in the divine Trinity. We are consciously now living "according
to the image and likeness" that is Jesus Christ. He is seen as an
abiding light living within us and in all things around us. His light
shines day and night within our hearts and in our intelligence. It
bathes us in his radiance and knows no setting. It is living and life-
giving, transforming into light those of us whom it illuminates.

This illumination by Jesus, however, does not mean that we have
to leave others to find God. It does not mean that we must stop
working in the inner city in order to find God in some ethereal,
spiritual otherworld where prayer in opposed to action. Nor does
love of God require spouses to give up, or inhibit, their love for
each other, for their children, for their neighbors. Teilhard de Chardin was fond of describing the presence of the risen Lord Jesus
inside of matter as the "diaphanous" shining of Christ from within
the material world of atoms and molecules, in movement toward
greater complexity and greater unity in consciousness.

Such a way of "seeing" God everywhere is a result of family
intimacy. Being able to recognize in people the passionate, loving
presence of the triune God, is a gift of grace, an effect of sacramental
causality. It comes to those who have embraced the crucified Lord
by dying to every form of self-centeredness. Spouses who see God
this way have entered into a true poverty of spirit, an adequate sense
of their creatureliness that identifies them as a man and a woman in
a "truthful" relationship with God and with other human beings
and the world around them. Only the Holy Spirit can enlighten
such Christians, through the faith that enables them to comprehend
the incomprehensible.

The Holy Spirit takes away the darkness from their minds and
fills them with a divine light revealing the inner life of the Trinity.
This uncreated gift bathes them much as the sun casts its warm rays
upon the whole world, making everything visible in its light. Spouses
see God in each other, as the Source of all life. He is energizing life.
He gives life to everyone and everything that is. God's presence as
providence extends to every little detail in the relationships of husband and wife to each other, to their children, to friends and all
other human beings they meet. But primarily, he is present in their
sacramental sexuality, in the self-abandonment that they achieve so

dramatically in sexual intercourse, but act out in every detail of their daily life as well.

Married persons come to understand that God has no mouth to speak; yet, they learn to hear God speak his Word as they listen to each other. God has no hand to grasp a man and a woman and to guide them, but such a husband and wife, transfigured by the in-dwelling Trinity, know that God touches them with his divine hand, in the touch of each other. God has no sexual body with which to desire passionately a consummated union with human beings; but husband and wife experience that passionate love of God as they desire to surrender themselves, through continuous love in every thought, word and deed, to each other.

TRANSFIGURING LOVE

Lips do not kiss, but two human beings in love do. Two bodies do not have sexual intercourse, but a husband and a wife do. They act out their total, permanent commitment in love toward each other in a body, soul and spirit intercourse. Such a conjugal act is done by human beings who act out their inner psychic and spiritual oneness through their two whole, embodied beings becoming one. When such an act involves the entire man and woman on all levels of their being, then they mutually transcend the limitations of the love they have already attained. Through this act, they are entering into the transfiguration of the glorified, risen Savior. They are, quite literally, making love.

In marital love, a man and a woman are gifted to love each other as God does, with God's very triune love loving within them. God's Spirit pours into them both a beautiful hope for what is yet unseen but could come to be, through the transfiguring process of marital love. Neither has yet experienced that good, noble or beautiful per-son that he can become; yet in the eyes of the lover, each spouse is already that lovable, unique person whose whole identity is in rela-tion to the beloved, and loving spouse.

For those who have learned to let go of their hold on their sepa-rate lives and have taken the risk of hoping in the goodness of the other by being "vulnerable" and open to serve the one loved, great riches of unifying love and prayer are opened up. A global presence of God that is distinct from the two loved ones and yet that can never be separated from them emerges in their lives. It is a beginning of heaven when two persons experience marital oneness, each one "bone from my bones, and flesh from my flesh" (Gen. 2:23). Through their union, they live a larger oneness with God. Such intimacy is the basic experience of Church, two persons forming a oneness in the Trinity.

In marital intimacy, we have a microcosm of society and of the entire universe. Christ is present in the universe, transforming humanity and even the subhuman cosmos into his very own Body, the Church. The same risen Jesus Christ is present in the lives of married persons, pouring into them the energies of triune love.

As they open themselves to his presence in their love, they gain strength to believe in the transfiguring power of God, who is infinitely beyond their own possibilities. For what is impossible to men is possible to God (Matt. 19:26; Gen. 18:14). They can believe that, out of their petty moods, carelessness and momentary lapses into self-centeredness, something beautiful can emerge. For each partner can transcend such crosses and deaths by being transfigured in the power of Divine Love, by the Spirit, to rise in hope to new loving and self-giving, to new trinitarian intimacy. Something of Christ's Taboric light is allowed by married people to pierce through the monotony and banality of each day, as they transcend the brokenness and frailty of their human situation. Hope touches the darkness of each perplexing doubt and momentary fear like a strong light. They see, in seeming obscurity, the glory of God.

COCREATORS OF THE WORLD IN CHRIST

Our of such mundane cares and worries, the loved ones call out in childlike trust for God to truly transform their love into new life. Their vision is one of finding God in the ordinary things of married life, thereby coming alive with creative powers. Unsuspected energies are released in the discovery of God in their mutual love. These pour out into the tasks of everyday living, now done with peace and joy. Such couples enter into each situation to bring forth their potential as people who are truly alive, working as a new creation to reconcile the world to the Father (2 Cor. 5:17–18). To cooperate with God in bringing forth new life, whether in their own children or in loving service toward others outside of the family, is to enter deeply into the mystery of God's great, creative love for his people, his children. Grace hurls married couples into an ecstasy that touches the center of God's active love and makes him truly felt, perhaps for the first time in their lives, as a loving, involved God who is not far away, "since it is in him that we live and move and exist" (Acts 17:28).

When husband and wife care for each other, ardently desiring to give themselves totally to each other in passionate love of total dedication and self-surrender, and think only in terms of loving service toward each other, their concern flows out to their children. A loving family will radiate the love of God toward their neighbors, reverenced for their uniqueness. Such a love, rooted in God's very own love for each of his children, will spread out in an openness to serve all human beings, whoever or wherever they may be.

CHANNELS OF TRANSFORMING LOVE TO OTHERS

Being holy is a continuous progress in love. It is a calling for all of us in the church—laity, clergy, religious. The Vatican Council II's *Constitution on the Church* declares this universal call to sanctity: "In the Church not everyone marches along the same path; yet all are called to sanctity and have obtained an equal privilege of faith through the justice of God" (II, 33). To the degree that married couples contemplate God in their conjugal love, to that degree they will actively be able to serve God in a return of love. True prayer is measured by our love for others in humble service. In the surrender of self to each other in loving union, spouses discover their own unique personhoods. Marriage can no longer be considered an obstacle to sanctity, or a distraction from intimacy with God. It is, instead, an instrument of that intimacy, a cause of sanctifying grace. Sexual intimacy, far from being shameful or selfish, is a sacrament— a symbolic cause, and causal symbol of trinitarian life in us.

This book has had as its purpose to suggest the lines of a Catholic spirituality of marriage in which marriage is a vocation in which two people gradually fall in love with each other and with the triune God simultaneously. It is the normal school for forming saints, truly realized human beings created and sanctified by Father, Son and Spirit, to live in love and to incarnate the love of God for all whom they meet and serve. Matrimony is a sacrament that builds the Church.

Selected Bibliography

Anzia, Joan Meyer, M.D., and Durkin, Mary G., D. Mn., *Marital Intimacy: A Catholic Perspective*. New York: Andrews and McMeel, Inc., 1980.

Beavers, W. Robert, and Kaslow, Florence W. "The Anatomy of Hope." *The Journal of Marital and Family Therapy* 7 (April, 1981), pp. 119–126.

Beavers, W. Robert. *Psychotherapy and Growth: A Family Systems Perspective*. New York: Brunner-Mazel Publishers, 1977.

Bernardin, Joseph Cardinal. "A Theology of Sexual Intimacy." *Origins* 10 (October 9, 1980), pp. 260–262.

Bronfenbrenner, Urie. *The Ecology of Human Development: Experiments by Nature and Design*. Cambridge, Massachusetts: Harvard University Press, 1979.

Bowen, Murray. *Family Therapy in Clinical Practice*. New York: Jason Aronson, 1978.

Chandler, Gail E. "The Family as Spiritual Community." Presentation at the workshop *Mystery and Mysticism*, Weston, Connecticut, April 3, 1979.

Cooke, Bernard J. *Christian Sacraments and Christian Personality*. New York: Holt, Rinehart and Winston, 1965.

Dicks, Henry V. *Marital Tensions: Clinical Studies Towards a Psychological Theory of Interaction*. New York: Basic Books, Inc., 1967.

Dominian, Jack. *Marriage, Faith and Love: A Basic Guide to Christian Marriage*. New York: The Crossroad Publishing Co., 1982.

Epstein, Joseph. *Divorced in America: Marriage in an Age of Possibility*. New York: E. P. Dutton and Co., 1974.

Erikson, Erik H. *Insight and Responsibility: Lectures on the Ethical Implications of Psychoanalytic Insight*. New York: W. W. Norton, Inc., 1964.

Framo, James L. "Family of Origin as a Therapeutic Resource for Adults in Marital and Family Therapy: You Can and Should Go Home Again." *Family Process* 15 (June, 1976), pp. 193–210.

Gallagher, Charles A., S.J. *One Flesh*. Dublin: Catholic Communications Institute, 1980.

_____ . *Parents Are Lovers*. Garden City: Doubleday and Co., Inc., 1977.

Greeley, Andrew M. *The Denominational Society*. Glenview, Illinois: Scott, Foresman, 1972.

_____ . *Sexual Intimacy*. New York: The Seabury Press, 1973.

Halpern, Howard. *Cutting Loose: An Adult Guide to Coming to Terms with Your Parents*. New York: Simon and Schuster, 1976.

John Paul II, Pope. *The Role of the Christian Family in the Modern World*. Vatican City: Polyglot Press.

Kaplan, Helen Singer. *Disorders of Sexual Desire and Other New Concepts and Techniques in Sex Therapy*. Vol. II *The New Sex Therapy*. New York: Brunner/Mazel Publishers, 1979.

Kennedy, Eugene C., and Heckler, Victor J. *The Catholic Priest in the United States: Psychological Investigations.* Washington, D.C.: United States Catholic Conference, 1972.

Lester, Gordon J. *When Love Seeks New Depths.* St. Meinrad, Indiana: Abbey Press, 1979.

Maloney, George A., S.J. *Invaded by God: Mysticism and the Indwelling Trinity.* Denville, New Jersey: Dimension Books, 1979.

Minuchin, Salvador. "Adolescence: Society's Response and Responsibility." *Adolescence* 4 (Winter, 1969), pp. 455–76.

Ricoeur, Paul. *The Symbolism of Evil.* Translated by Emerson Buchanan. New York: Harper and Row, 1967.

Satir, Virginia. *Conjoint Family Therapy: A Guide to Theory and Technique.* rev. ed. Palo Alto, California: Science and Behavior Books, Inc., 1967.

Sawin, Margaret. "Growing Through Family Clusters." *Marriage and Family Living* 64 (April, 1982), pp. 18–20.

Stafford, Bishop J. Francis. "The Marriage Covenant." *Origins* 10 (October 30, 1980), pp. 317–318.

Stoller, Robert J. *Perversion.* New York: Pantheon. 1975.

Turk, James L. "Power as the Achievement of Ends: A Problematic Approach in Family and Small Group Research." *Family Process* 13 (March, 1974), pp. 39–52.

Wilczak, Paul F., ed. *Marriage Enrichment.* St. Meinrad, Indiana: Abbey Press. 1979. (Includes Wilczak's "The Fullness of Physical Love" and his review of Karol Wojtyla's *Love and Responsibility.*)

Williamson, Donald S. "New Life at the Graveyard: A Method of Therapy for Individuation from a Dead Former Parent." *Journal of Marriage and Family Counseling* (January, 1978), pp. 90–112.

Wojtyla, Karol (Pope John Paul II). *Love and Responsibility.* Translated by H. T. Willetts. New York: Farrar, Straus, and Giroux, 1981.

Yankelovich, Daniel. "New Rules in American Life: Searching for Self-Fulfillment in a World Turned Upside Down." *Psychology Today* 15 (April, 1981), pp. 35–95.

Zinn, Grover A. *Richard of St. Victor.* The Classics of Western Spirituality. New York: Paulist Press, 1979.

(For a more extensive bibliography, see Evelyn Eaton and James D. Whitehead, *Marrying Well,* New York: Doubleday and Co., Inc., 1981).